HOW TO BE DEEP DOWN FOREVER HAPPY

BY

TOM GNAGEY

The Family of Man Press

///

SECTION ONE:

CHAPTER ONE
The Journey's First Step

THE BUILDING BLOCKS

When I was a boy, I was restless beyond anything that might be considered reasonable. When I went to get my hair cut, the barber, a savvy father of seven sons, would hand me a wooden, Chinese, puzzle. I'd work on it diligently (and apparently quietly) while he attended to my locks. I was always taken by the fact that each of those puzzles seemed so difficult - so impossible - so unsolvable - right up until that magical instant when I uncovered the secret. From then on it was no challenge whatsoever - a piece of cake, as we used to say.

This book will show you how the search for Happiness is a lot like those Chinese puzzles. Once you know and accept the secret, life simply becomes and stays fantastic!

Good fortune shined on me early in life. I discovered, or learned, or happened upon the secret of Happiness - not just moment to moment happiness like comes with lollipops or winning a race or getting a bike or a big house - but Deep Down Forever Happiness that has nothing whatsoever to do with the accumulation of stuff, money, power, fame, or prestige. The former is so often dangerously confused with the latter that it will take us a number of pages to sort it all out.

Later.

As a youngster, I watched so many people struggle with sadness and discontent - the blues we called it. I watched so many people, (kids, grownups, other kids' parents, teachers) burst forth in uncontrollable anger. I watched so many people express frustration at their job or at a life situation that was fully unsatisfying. I wondered why they allowed such things to take control of them and keep happiness at bay. I wondered how they had missed the secret when it seemed so obvious.

I need to get personal, here, so you can understand how the basic secret of happiness rubbed off on me.

I was the third – by eight years – in a family of three boys. Mom was not employed outside the home. Dad was the school superintendent. Teachers were near the bottom of the heap when it came to income. Still, I never considered us poor.

I was astounded the first time I heard my family referred to as poor - I was six. How could we be poor when we had everything we needed? I absolutely could not figure out how such a mistake had been made. I had three shirts and two pairs of pants (school and church) and there were always clean underwear and sox in my drawer when I opened it mornings. I had a winter coat, and boots for snow and rain. I got a pair of new shoes every September for school and could absolutely not understand why a kid would need any shoes at all in the summer - well, except for Sunday mornings.

There was always a wide variety of delicious food to eat and very special sweet bits which came my way after I cleaned my plate. When I wanted something, I didn't have - a wagon, a bike, a telescope - I often figured out how to make it, scrounged the parts, and went about creating it.

One of my early 'Aha! Epiphanies' came when I was eight. I remember verbalizing it to my parents. "I feel so sorry for the poor rich kids who have to just go out and buy the things they want. They miss out on all the planning and building and the fun that goes with it." (Paraphrased, I'm sure. I also realize it was a simpler time and that building a new video game for oneself from the leavings in the city dump is probably not a current day possibility. Still, the essence of that enlightenment really does remain true as we will discover together, here.)

Back to my Happy family. Ten percent of what we earned - my lawn mowing and snow shoveling included - gladly went into the 'Help Jar'. We spent Sunday afternoons doing things for others - people in need. Dad and I repaired and painted picket fences and porch floors and railings. We spaded and planted gardens and flower beds. I mowed grass and raked leaves. Mom cleaned and cooked and chatted with lonely older folks or baby sat for new parents so they could have the afternoon just to themselves - take in a movie or spread a picnic in the park.

Saturday evenings while still at the supper table, we planned the next day's activities and counted the Help money to see how much we had available to spend on the projects - if any was needed for paint or seeds or supplies of some kind.

While carrying out the projects it always felt so good to know I was being helpful. Later on, it felt good to remember about the activities. In those ways, it presented a continuing source of Happiness (and does to this day, in fact).

Dad held two firm beliefs about being helpful. I pass them on to you as food for thought.

First, our joy has to come from the process and the result of being helpful, and never from being thanked or coming to think highly of ourselves for what we did. ("I helped, and that makes me feel good," never, "I helped and that proves I'm a good and worthy guy!")

Second, whenever possible, we did our helping anonymously. His point was that when the doer benefits in some way (other than gaining personal satisfaction and Happiness) it is not a true act of charity. It changes the focus from being helpful to one's own personal gain. "I donate $100 to the Salvation Army and show up to be thanked at the public banquet. Then I go home and make sure to deduct it from my taxes." Not Charity, my Dad would have said. (Not that the money couldn't be put to good use.) Instead, it would illustrate pure and simple self-serving behavior and motivation - basking in the public thanks and accompanying adulation so others will think well of you, and then, benefiting from the financial gain of the tax deduction. In his mind, it would be a flat-out instance of buying attention, status, and financial advantage for yourself.

This illustrates one of the most ineffective ways to go about finding Happiness - consciously setting out to make other people like you or think well of you. Live your life according to a positive social philosophy, be true to it, and you WILL be Happy with yourself. You can't find deep down Happiness until you are satisfied - Happy - about yourself. (Not about your stuff or power or status.) Then you'll find it really won't matter what others think about you. You only ever really need to have your own approval to be Deep Down Forever Happy. In fact, you HAVE to have your own approval in order to be Deep Down Forever Happy. Find those things you dislike about yourself, banish them, and replace them with acceptable traits using the powerful technique this book will show you, and you're nearly there.

Stating the underlying secret without furnishing the necessary framework and background may make it seem frivolous and naive - over-simplified, for sure. I'll risk that here if you'll promise to examine the presentation further.

Deep Down Happiness begins with taking good care of yourself, your loved ones, and your neighbors, and doing so eagerly, just because you really want to, all in accordance with a positive personal and social philosophy.

That immediately requires the definitions of things such as care, good care, yourself, loved ones, neighbors, philosophy. It requires answers to how Happiness depends on these things. It requires a brand-new perspective for many folks who have been living their lives believing it is the stuff or money or power or prestige one has that is the basis for Happiness. It never has been, and in order to make sense of it all, this book breaks the basic secret down into twelve parts.

Reading on, you will explore several important areas related to solving the Happiness puzzle. You will have an advantage over my situation back as the lad in the barber's chair because I'm going to give you the solutions - the secrets - up front. I'm going to tell you exactly what to do and how to do it.

Allow me one final analogy using the wooden puzzles. Even though I can tell you that the secret is to pull out all the yellow cubes and push in all the red ones, that secret will do you absolutely no good until you actually do that pushing and pulling - take the suggested steps - yourself. Knowing the secrets to Happiness will be of no use to you if you don't try them, practice them, and regularly implement them. I urge you to complete the exercises, here, as they are presented.

BOOKS, PROGRAMS AND MANUALS
They are different in important ways.

When setting out to present information aimed at changing or improving some part of the human experience, an author has several approaches at his disposal.

The first is to write a Book (and browsing any bookstore will demonstrate that it seems a million, self-help, authors have done just that). Books typically take one of two forms. Some entertain (novels) and others present information (textbooks, self-help, history, or some aspect of current affairs, for example). They are based on the premise that the reader (not thought of as a user) will capably do as he or she pleases with the content.

Programs are far more complex sets of activities that usually involve a combination of some reading (a book or manual), some listening (tape or CD), some watching (video or live presentations) and some participation (group meetings, lectures, and so on). Programs are meant to handle more involved, complex, and difficult material or topics.

Manuals (like this one) resemble both the book (it provides information) and the program (it is arranged in such a way to help the participant practice new ways of doing things). Manuals can be huge, involved, and time consuming or they can be simple, short, and self-evident. My intention and hope is for this manual to be the latter - simple, short, to the point, and self-evident.

I suggest that you approach this manual slowly and deliberately. Read one chapter, take a day to work on the exercise, and then re-read the chapter before moving on. Another useful approach is to read the entire book first to determine where you are going and then start again from the beginning following the plan above. (I highly recommend the first approach.)

THE SECRETS

The rest of this book will present, examine, and illustrate my Secrets for Deep Down Forever Happiness. There will be suggested activities, which you can perform to satisfy yourself about the truth of each secret.

If you are less happy than you want to be, you may, at first glance, find suggestions here that will seem foreign to you - strange, odd, or even uncomfortable to think about. That makes sense, of course. If these are the secrets to Happiness, and if you are not happy, you've clearly been missing some things. You may have even been outright rejecting them as you have been unknowingly pursuing a path into unhappiness. It will be necessary for you to open your mind far enough to hear me out.

Below, is a list of the basic secrets in shortened form. The following chapters will define and develop each topic. You will be shown how to practice each step so you can determine for yourself the truth it holds.

SECRET 1- Never expect your Deep Down Forever Happiness to flow from stuff, money, power, fame, or winning. (Deep Down Happiness is absolutely free and non-competitive in nature!)

SECRET 2- Find, understand, and practice a positive social philosophy (giving not taking, helping not hurting, creating not criticizing).

SECRET 3- Live a life of integrity (always living up to your own positive value system).

SECRET 4- You only ever really need to have your own approval to be Deep Down Happy.

SECRET 5- Expand tendencies toward Altruism and rid yourself of Selfism (will be defined later).

SECRET 6- Routinely (daily) take good care of yourself

and those with whom you come in contact. Begin by reducing gruffness and isolation and increasing kindness and interest.

SECRET 7- Replace worrying with planning.

SECRET 8- Replace the always destructive, go nowhere, 'Blame and punish', mental set, with the usually helpful, 'What needs to be fixed?' technique.

SECRET 9- Take positive steps to get rid of the harmful, unnecessary, negative beliefs and tendencies (directives), hiding in the depths of your mind, and replace them with positive, useful, directives. (A simple, powerful method will be presented.)

SECRET 10- See each error you make or failure you experience as a positive event that you can use to improve your life. (You have at that point learned what not to do next time.)

SECRET 11- In general, only relate and dwell on good things about people. Build folks up. Avoid pointing out (gossiping) or dwelling on anybody's faults (including your own).

SECRET 12- Downsize the stuff in your life. If you bought it mainly to 'make' yourself feel good (happy), or important, or better than somebody else, get rid of it!!! (As you will see, this doesn't mean you can't have and do things that bring you enjoyment.)

EXERCISE ONE:
Background

How often have we been told to just relax about such and such?   That directive seldom works because it is misworded. A more useful phrasing would be: Relax so you can think more clearly about such and such.

The mind and body affect each other every second of our existence. It is as if maintaining a state of tension sucks energy away from our constructive thinking processes. Here is a formula that is almost always true.

Thinking about a Problem + Tension = Panic (nonconstructive thinking)

Here's another one:

Thinking about a Problem + Relaxation = Ability to concentrate (constructive thinking)

As you progress through this material it will become more and more essential that you master the processes of physical relaxation. If you already have a system with which you are comfortable you may want to go with that one. If not, or if you're interested in expanding your horizons, try this one.

Exercise

Sit or recline so you are comfortable. (Prone, head on a flat pillow, is best at the outset.) Arrange for a comfortable temperature. Loosen or remove tight or binding clothing. Let your eyes close naturally and gently. The essence of this exercise is to systematically relax every major muscle system in your body. The basic process will be to first tense an area (like your toes and feet), take a moment to notice how that tension feels and then relax those muscles. You will repeat it several times - tensing, holding, noticing, and relaxing. After several repetitions let the muscle system remain relaxed naming the experience ("Feet and toes relaxed") over and over again as you reduce the muscle tension even further. Then, move on the next area. Practice relaxing in this order. Toes, Feet, Ankles, Lower Legs, Knees, Upper Legs, Hips, Buttocks, Right side back, Left side back, Right shoulder, Left Shoulder, Chest, Abdomen, Upper right arm, Upper left arm, Elbows, Lower arms, wrists, Hands and fingers.

As you practice try to get a mind's eye picture of the body part you are relaxing. As you relax each muscle set, smile - just a crack of a smile. The Deep Mind often takes its cue from the state of the body. Smiles and frowns send powerful messages to the Deep Mind. A smile tells it, "THIS is how I want to be unless there is some good reason to be otherwise." Eventually you will be able to produce instant, full body, relaxation by merely cracking a small-scale smile.

There is another important use you will make of this state of deep relaxation. Tension builds a wall between you and your usually hidden Deep Mind. (I know. It sounds strange. In this case think of "you" as being your Conscious Mind - the part you are aware of as you think and go about your daily life.) Very soon, you will learn how to manage your Deep Mind - removing directives you don't want and adding those you do want. In order to communicate with your Deep Mind, you must lower the level of general body tension so you can gain access. (It is really not a magical as it may appear!)

So, practice at least once a day. Several times will allow more rapid progress. The ultimate aim is to achieve virtually instantaneous, body relaxation on your command.

I routinely relax dozens of time every day. It keeps me focused and mentally alert and effective. My routine takes about ten seconds. Here is how I do it. I close my eyes (I'm usually sitting). I exhale, forcefully, emptying my lungs completely. Then, as I inhale, I say and visualize the sequence of letters, R-E-L-A. I hold the breath a few seconds and then as I slowly exhale and relax, I say and visualize the final letter, X. If you try that right now, I'm quite sure you will feel an immediate sense of increased relaxation. Just imagine how wonderful it will feel once you have practiced utilizing that mind-body connection for a month or so!

CHAPTER TWO
The Necessary Path

Deep Down Forever Happiness does not just happen. We don't wake up one day and there it is. Like most things that are worthwhile, Deep Down Forever Happiness requires working a plan - a plan, which is broken down into a logical sequence of easily attainable steps, each one dependent upon the successful mastery of those that came before.

Although this characterization requires work and effort on your part it does, because of that, define Happiness as a state over which you have control. It is not willy-nilly. It is not haphazard. It is not a matter of luck or circumstances into which you are born or fall. Deep Down Forever Happiness is always* within YOUR control.

[*There are some conditions of inadequate or ineffective brain chemicals and processes or other body function irregularities that seem to dull or even prevent this state, but most of those can be regulated medically. If you find yourself in such a severe, habitual, situation, begin by getting the necessary medical help. Understand, however, that reducing or eliminating depression or fear or anger with a pill or other therapy is only the starting point. A follow-up plan to achieve lasting Happiness is still required. One like that presented in these pages should help.]

Here at the outset I will lay out seven concepts that necessarily contribute to Happiness. [As you may have surmised by this point, when spelled with a capital 'H', the term Happiness refers to Deep Down Forever Happiness. When spelled with a lower case 'h' happiness refers to the more momentary, fleeting, and less significant pleasant experiences that many folks pursue in their unsuccessful struggle to find Happiness.] More than just the basis for Happiness, I believe these concepts represent the necessary foundation for Peace - Peace within relationships, families, neighborhoods, and between differing philosophic bastions, and countries.

In grade school, we were once given an assignment to write an essay on achieving World Peace. My classmates all took stances which were negative in nature. They dwelled on things such as "Stop such and such," or "Put people in jail when they do such and such," or "Make it illegal to say bad things about the government," Or "Force everybody to stop hurting each other." My flesh crawled. To me, their suggestions were not peace inducing suggestions. They were merely another version of un-peace. Forcing others to change and punishing them if they didn't.

My thesis was simple: True peace equals a state in which all people are regularly and sincerely engaged in helping the other people in their lives become and remain safe, healthy, helpful, and happy. (We had often talked about it at home.) I simplified the process for achieving it with this characterization: neighbors helping neighbors. * It seemed sensible, realistic, foolproof, and simple to me. Everybody is somebody's neighbor, and everybody has a neighbor. My teacher wrote her comment: "Naive but fascinating."

[* Later, I expanded on the 'peace concept' in my book, Everything I needed to know about saving the world I learned before I was ten.]

Let me now spend a few pages laying the basis for the seven steps. In my mind, I imagine them as a path containing several Ys. At each Y, I must keep to the trail that leads to the proper next required step. The following diagram sets the stage but will only be truly meaningful after the discussion below. The path begins with the most basic kinds of data we human beings encounter.

PERCEIVED EXPERIENCES
(Reality - the real world - as you come to see it)

DEEP MIND DIRECTIVES
(Sets your habitual response patterns based on your perceptions)

PHILOSOPHY
(Sets outlook on life and your necessary place and roles in society)

INTENTIONS
(Sets ones behavioral, interaction, potentials)

ACTIONS
(Sets personality and social interaction styles)

INTEGRITY
(Sets the only truly stable, healthy, mental state)

HAPPINESS
(Sets long-term state of inner comfort and personal satisfaction)

PEACE
(Sets the stable path leading to mankind's comfortable and productive survival.)

Let us now examine each step in more detail.

Perceived Experiences and
Deep Mind Directives:
I suppose we've all had experiences similar to this. You and several others are traveling in a vehicle. You all spot something in the ditch to your left as you pass by.
"See that dead cat?"

"It wasn't a cat it was a rubber boot."

"No, it wasn't. It was part of a tire."

All three passengers saw the same object. Each passenger experienced a different image - a different interpretation of reality. Each believed that what he had seen was the 'real' thing and that the others had been wrong.

Perceived experience is just that - your personalized interpretation of what goes on about you. It may be images, as in the example, or it may be statements heard or questions asked or facial expressions or body language you witness. Regardless of the source, you make an interpretation and tuck it away inside your brain - mind, actually. [The term 'mind' refers to all the processes that take place inside the brain - thoughts, we often call them, though we are really not aware of many things that go on 'in' the mind.]

The deepest part of your mind has but one purpose – to serve your best interests, so, it is eager to believe your interpretation of things and once it has stored one of your impressions it becomes difficult to modify it. Even if you later change an interpretation of something ("Yes. I can see now that it was probably a boot."), that new impression does not automatically replace the old one; it just stores a new – additional - impression. They sit there in the mind as generally equally strong impressions although the last one stored typically is acted upon more frequently. Still, either one is likely to come to mind as you try to remember.

"Mother takes good care of me when I'm sick"

"Mother hurts me when she doesn't like what I've done."

"Mother pays attention to me."

"Mother pays more attention to my brother than she does to me."

"Mother says no candy before supper."

"Mother sometimes gives me candy before supper."

Multiply those stored images of mother by a million and you can begin to see the problem the Deep Mind has when you ask it to characterize 'mother' for you.

I said the most recent deposit into the Deep Mind is typically the one it brings up for you. Although most likely, it is not always true. Images (ideas, responses, etc.) that are placed into the Deep Mind along with intense emotion tend to be the most powerful of all images stored there regardless of elapsed time. So, one severe beating may over-ride all of the more loving images. Happily, the positive images of mother tend to overwhelm the negative emotions stored as a result of the occasional spanking or grounding. Not always, however!

I'm not picking on mothers. They are just such easy picking. Few experience sources are more important in the development of the Deep Mind than is the early interaction with one's mother.

The point in all this is that people live their lives largely according to the Deep Mind Directives that they and others have set there. Directives are based on how things have been perceived - your view of reality at some moment. Sometimes that view is just dead wrong, so unrealistic directives develop and help guild one's life in inappropriate directions. Small children accept what they are told without question. They literally suck in Directives. Directives set in that way can be helpful, at least in the short term. They can also be harmful in the long run! (More later.)

Most of a person's Deep Mind directives are helpful (or at least benign). Some of them are not helpful. Still others are devastating. Happiness will never be achieved when there are Deep Mind Directives sitting there forcing one to be unhappy. Later in the book you will learn specific techniques for finding and ridding yourself of such harmful, Deep Mind, directives. It is necessary to understand and accept several basic concepts before those techniques can be helpful. When you remove a harmful directive, you must usually replace it with a helpful directive. They will be constructed from the information and ideas you will learn in the next hundred or so pages.

Remember, the mind acts on what it thinks it perceives. That is the mind's reality. When it mis-perceives events, or intentions, or emotional responses, it has to base its reactions and memories on that mis-perception. As children, understandably unskilled in making such interpersonal judgments, we often misinterpret words and deeds and it is those inappropriate interpretations - beliefs - that sit in our Deep Minds directing our reactions and memories. Often, they need to be fixed - removed or replaced - before we can find Happiness.

PHILOSOPHY:
Without belaboring the topic, (the way philosophers might do) let's think about a persons' philosophy of life (social philosophy) in two dimensions. First, a social philosophy is either based in ME or US. Second, it is either POSITIVE (building) or NEGTIVE (destructive). Happiness stems from 'US' melded with 'POSITIVE'. Any other combination of those four elements has to result in unhappiness - in terms of Deep Down Forever Happiness. See the diagram below.

POSITIVE   NEGATIVE
                        ME   Positive Me
Negative Me

                        US   Positive Us
Negative Us

Think about these questions.

> Who are easier to live with: happy people or sad people?

> Who are easier to live with: healthy people or sick people?

> Who are easier to live with: law abiding people or law-breaking people?

> Who are easier to live with: people who can meet their own financial needs or those who cannot meet their own financial needs?

> Who are easier to live with: people who live in safety or those who live in fear of harm?

> Who are easier to live with: people who demonstrate that they care about your welfare or people whose behaviors

suggest they only really care about their own welfare?

My guess is you would describe the easy to live with person as happy, healthy, law abiding, financially self-sufficient, fear free, and one who cares about your welfare and actively seeks to maintain and/or improve it. Does that describe you? If so, Happiness can't be far away.

I further imagine that you would describe the hard to live with person as one who is often sad, openly exhibits and/or complains about his physical maladies, breaks the law, unnecessarily depends on the dole for support, lives in fear for his safety, and really only cares about and takes care of himself. Does that even in part describe you? If so, you have some work to do.

Happy people tend to see, emphasize, and acknowledge the best in others and the world, without denying the darker side of life. They take action to improve lives - their own and others (US). Unhappy people tend to dwell on the worst, the unpleasant, and the darker side of things and generally deny the positive potential of the human species. They take no steps to improve the lot of mankind and may even attempt to attack and harm others. The basic secret for Happiness is ridding oneself of the latter traits and replacing them with the former.

In general conversation, Happy people are heard building other people up and expressing delight in others good fortune and potential - never presenting or rehashing their problems and negative gossip. Happy people are not complainers. They meet problems with suggestions and efforts to reasonably solve them rather than search for somebody to blame or put down. Unhappy people are filled with dark gossip, innuendo, and finger pointing (blaming). Pointing out other people's faults may be their only way to make themselves look or feel adequate.

The negative aspects demonstrated by the 'unhappys' in the world, as well as the positive traits of the 'happys' are both based in, and fostered by, Deep Mind Directives. Change the directives, and you change the state of mind - it really is that simple. [After you finish this manual you may want to read in more depth about the Deep Mind. See my book titled, Deep Mind Mastery, concise edition. Directives and philosophy intermesh - they are interdependent - they influence each other. A basic part of any pathway toward happiness is establishing a positive, 'US' based philosophy that reaches out to include, assist, and approach others.

Establishing such a philosophy is no big deal. Evaluate each of the ways in which you deal with others in terms of the two dimensions - US vs Me and Positive vs Negative. For those behaviors that are clearly not US-Positive, find ways for modifying them. One example of a positive philosophy can be found in, Building a Positive Philosophy: Personal and Social, by this author. Positive philosophies tend to suggest what one should do rather than what one should not do.

Warning: No matter how positive and sensible a philosophy may appear and no matter how much you truly want to embrace it and live your life by it, if it goes against any major, contrary, Deep Mind Directives, the philosophy will not work for you. (Take New Year's Resolutions or dieting, as simple-minded examples.)

See the progression down the path, so far. Perceived Experiences are the basis for Deep Mind Directives. Deep Mind Directives are the basic regulators of our characteristic, day to day, philosophy (regardless of what we may think we want it to be). Next you will see how that working philosophy dictates our Intentions - what we are trying to accomplish in life.

INTENTIONS:

My mother always said it was important to believe the best about people until they proved otherwise. (Suppose I just might have tucked away a Deep Mind directive related to that!) She was really referring to the intentions of other people. The first part of her saying could be restated this way: Believe others are acting according to their good intentions even when things don't turn out all that great, until . . .

Denise the Menace is chuck full of good intentions, but the results are often not stellar, are they? Does he intend to make Mr. Wilson's life unhappy? Just the opposite. His underlying intention is always to make it wonderful!

Intentions characterize our potential behaviors. It might be said that we really are what we intend to be and not always what we seem to be. When what we intend to be and what we seem to be to others are pretty much the same, we project a genuineness that feels comfortable all the way around.

Sometimes, however, things get in the way and we are unable to demonstrate our good intentions. For example, we may harbor deep seated fears that prohibit us from building the kinds of positive relationships we want to have (intend to have).

Our intentions reflect the Deep Mind Directives that are typically dominant. When that collective is generally positive, we are motivated by positive (helpful) intentions. When that collective is generally negative, we are motivated by negative (destructive or at least non-helpful or unpleasant) intentions.

The Deep Mind has one overriding, basic, Prime Directive (intention): Keep my person alive. Only a very few situations or beliefs can override that. (Protecting your child in the face of your own certain death or injury, for example.) When our best intentions seldom seem to guide our behaviors, the first place to look is for some connection between that prime, survival, directive, and how it may be keeping you from acting as you would like to. You want to make friends but can't. Perhaps that prime directive has been configured in such a way as to say almost everyone is dangerous or hurtful or untrustworthy. That keeps you from approaching or befriending others. There will be more about this later on.

Because of the nature of the Prime Directive (keep you safe at all costs) the Deep Mind is always at least skeptical if not downright untrusting of much that goes on around you. Until it is convinced things are safe, it keeps you cautious. It may tell you to hold back when strangers approach - not knowing if they are friendly or not. It may tell you to distrust all green-eyed people because as a baby a green-eyed sitter hurt you. You get the idea.

Although all Deep Minds are based on caution that doesn't mean they are all based on fear. When one is based on fear it motivates you (gives you intentions) to avoid or destroy things rather than to approach and accept things. "Don't go near bodies of water." "Don't expose your feelings." "Don't leave the house until you're beautiful." Think how different a person's intentions will be when a Deep Mind is based on trust, instead. Using sensible caution, approach strangers and see if you will like them for friends. Volunteer for a very difficult assignment, unafraid of the prospect of failure, because you are eager to learn whatever the experience has to teach you. Jump at the chance to go to a new camp because you trust yourself and others to make it a good time.

If you find that you are consistently unable to live up to your good intentions, it is likely due to a conflict between 'warring' directives (intentions). A fear-based Deep Mind has to be a closed, defensive, mind. It mistrusts everything until proven safe beyond any reasonable doubt (which will seldom happen). A trust-based Deep Mind leaves one open to new ideas and possibilities. If you want your children to be free to consider new possibilities, refrain from filling their Deep Minds with no-no's and don'ts and I'll beat or disown you if you do this or believe that. Instead, use phrases such as you might consider this, I want you to do it this way until you have sufficient experience to try it some other way, Nice try - how might you go about it so things turn out better next time?

Clearly, raising healthy Deep Minds is not all this black and white, but these examples suggest the essential plan. The more basic point is that the Deep Mind Directives you set inside a child early on will sit there to guide him for most of his life. It is very important to make as sure as you can that they will serve him well during his life in an unknowable, unpredictable, future. Those who are free to adapt reasonably to the changes will do best - have the best chances at Happiness. Those who are not free to change and adapt will most certainly fail and endure some level of perpetual unhappiness.

ACTIONS:

So, the way we perceive and interpret what goes on around us sets a number of directives into our Deep Mind.

Those directives (Deep Mind beliefs) determine the way we think about our place in the world and our relationships with others. When organized, this becomes our philosophy - specifically our social philosophy. Those same Deep Mind Directives form our intentions - the ideas about life and living it, that guide the way we act and react. They influence the things we want to have and the things we want to do. The things we actually do, are our actions, and they set the behavioral pattern that characterize us as people. We act nicely. We act hesitantly. We act aggressively. We act boldly. We act in accordance with our community's expectations, or we don't. And, on and on.

By studying another's actions - behaviors - for just a short time it becomes evident whether he is happy or not happy. For each of us, however, there is an intermediary step that defines whether or not we have achieved Deep Down Forever Happiness. That, I call Integrity.

INTEGRITY:

Look the word up in a dictionary and you'll find synonyms such as honesty, intactness, wholeness, soundness, perfection. As used here, Integrity simply means how well one's behavior corresponds to one's positive, social philosophy. In other words, how well do our day to day actions reflect our basic beliefs about how we should be acting? A high correlation suggests Integrity and Happiness. A low correlation suggests disorder or poor connectivity between philosophy and actions. One does not reflect the other. That inevitably produces disruptive tension and underlying unhappiness.

Without Integrity - a match between one's positive social philosophy and one's behavior - Deep Down Forever Happiness is absolutely impossible.

It raises several interesting scenarios. It is possible that one could 'fake' behaving like an upstanding citizen, or be one through fear of punishment and yet, because his Deep Mind Directives are negative, he is still unhappy - no match. (That can be fixed!) One might have a match between negative Deep Mind Directives and the despicable lifestyle they dictate and still be unhappy - the world does not treat such a person with kindness, freedom, and trust, so deep down Happiness will remain forever elusive.

HAPPINESS:

Happiness follows from a Deep Mind that is set with a preponderance of positive, responsible, directives; a positive social philosophy and the intentions it produces; actions that are helpful and comfortable to those around you; and the integrity of (the match between) a positive philosophy and behaviors.

In short, if you can fall asleep every night knowing that day you did (actions) your best to make a positive difference in the lives of others (positive social philosophy) you reaffirm your integrity and enjoy the wonderful wash of Deep Down, Forever, Happiness.

PEACE:

The one directive all Deep Minds share is the prime directive - keep my person safe. When a Deep Mind can in general believe it is safe, it has no reason to be either standoffish (preemptively cautious) or aggressive (self-protective) against others. When the world is filled with people of integrity - people living their positive social philosophy, Happy people - there are no threats, so peace prevails.

It is unrealistic to believe that every mind in the world will ever be Deep Down Forever Happy in the way I've described. The hope is that a large enough majority will be and therein jointly provide a deterrent to aggression, violence, and war.

Peace begins way back at the level of those Deep Mind Directives that we set into the minds of children, and on our ability as adults to spot and replace the dangerous, malevolent Directives in our own minds with positive, beneficial, Directives. Within the system presented in these pages, individual Happiness equals the only potential for the wider condition of genuine, enduring, world-wide, Peace.

Peace is that state in which the vast majority of people are engaged in helping other people regardless of individual differences. It seems so logical. People who are safe, well cared for, and financially secure enough, are easy to live with (peaceable). Those who are fearful, poorly cared for, financially stressed, are difficult to live with. It has to follow then that when we all help each other attain and maintain positive life situations we not only improve their chances at happiness, but we improve our own.

This author is not a Pollyanna. I understand that in a world of Deep Down Forever Happy people there may still be factions that want to destroy others who hold different views - most often religious, sometimes political or territorial. Those factions typically teach hate in well planned, systematic, ways, so their Deep Minds and those of their children are filled with violent, destructive, specifically targeted, Directives. They have no motivation to modify them. Their position and belief system depend on them. Then there is the occasional malevolent megalomaniac (Hitler) that comes onto the international scene. Still, the bottom line is that the more, Happy people, we have in this world the less chance that such contrary, destructive, movements can be successful.

EXERCISE
        1- Continue to practice relaxation.
        2- Getting a sense about what's right within your Deep Mind.
        Eventually you will inventory those things about your Deep Mind that suggest it isn't entirely the way you want it to be. First, however, it is essential to get a really good feel for what it Right about your Deep Mind.
        One way of doing this is to keep a list as you go through your days. On it enter the things you've done (your behaviors) for or with others that demonstrate to you that you are one of the good guys. Things you did that were intended to make others feel good about themselves. Things that made them smile. The mere act of smiling or nodding or speaking a short greeting to those you pass. Being helpful. Offering your assistance. Any thoughtful act. You get the idea. The sooner you can get them onto your list after they happen the better.

The Deep Mind works best with close proximity.

You may want to carry a pocket-sized note pad or just fold a sheet of printer paper in thirds the long way and then in half the other way. It provides a fairly firm surface and if you write small, it will hold a lot.

Have a wonderfully positive, list making, day!

SECTION TWO: The Secrets

CHAPTER THREE
SECRET 1
Deep Down Forever Happiness Stems from Integrity, not Stuff

We have heard the stories way too often: apparently successful, rich, famous, beautiful people having to check into rehab centers or taking their own lives. Happy people don't need or use drugs and certainly don't take their own lives. Did the success, fame, wealth, or physical appearance of those people provide Deep Down Forever Happiness for them? Clearly not.

Let me state it once more then go into more detail. The accumulation of stuff, money, power, prestige, or fame cannot provide Deep Down Forever Happiness. PERIOD! If you're headed down that path name it "Disappointment Trail" and hurry off at the first exit. Those things may provide some avenues for momentary enjoyment but NEVER confuse the two. Momentary enjoyment - even a long string of momentary enjoyments - is NOT a source for long term Happiness.

Can rich people, powerful people, beautiful people, famous people, be Happy? Of course, they can, but it is not tied to their riches, fame, power, or beauty.

Sam Walton is a case in point. He was a fine example of someone who had mastered Deep Down Forever happiness, but he had mastered it long before he became wealthy. (I know that for a fact because I was his stock boy in 1955.) He and his wife, Helen, never really appeared to be comfortable living like wealthy people. They didn't need to. They weren't depending on their wealth for happiness in their private lives because they already had the secret: interact in mutually helpful ways with those you come in contact.

There are other notable examples: Paul Newman and Joanne Woodward. Kirk Cameron, Jimmy Carter, Oprah Winfrey, Paul Harvey, Roy Rogers, and on down a long list. But, look at the history of any one of them and you will immediately understand that position, power, wealth, or stuff played no role in their Deep Down Forever Happiness.

Often, when we see someone's obvious good fortune and their apparent Happiness, our Deep Mind is likely to make an erroneous conclusion - that the good fortune caused or allowed the Happiness.

[The Deep Mind works by making correlation's - not by logic - and it often gets us into deep trouble because of it. Remember my reference to that green-eyed baby-sitter who hurt a child and the tike grew up angry at every green-eyed person he came across. He didn't know why, of course, but his Deep Mind had made that correlation and set it into his mind with all the strong emotion which accompanied the original pain. It remained a forceful (even though fully inaccurate and misleading) Deep Mind Directive. Most of us carry some of those and we need to find them and get rid of them. I'll show you how a bit later.]

Am I suggesting you shouldn't seek wealth or fame or other good fortune? No. I'm not. What I am saying is that if your reason for seeking those things is to make yourself Deep Down Forever Happy, you are on the wrong track and can only end up a disappointed and unhappy individual. Get happy first! Then, go seeking after whatever else you want. I really like wealthy, Deep Down Forever Happy people because they universally give huge portions of their wealth to worthwhile charities and funds that help needy folks survive and grow and become healthy, independent, and happier. Truly happy people almost never horde their good fortune - they don't need to. It is fully irrelevant in terms of their

Happiness. It makes them Happier to spread it around.

So, get Happy, get wealthy if you want, and spread it around. If you don't find yourself using it for the benefit of others, you'll know you really haven't yet achieved Deep Down Forever Happiness.

When young adults are polled about what they really want in life, two things almost always top the list - Happiness and Success (by several names). For some, Success is sought because it is believed that will provide Happiness. (Do I think it will?)

Success is an interesting concept because it holds shades of difference for each of us. For me, seeing how my own Happiness allows good things to spread out to those around me - like the ripples from a stone dropped in a quiet pond - represents Success. To Ray, an acquaintance, success means promotions at work and the raises that accompany them. For Dan and Joyce, buying a million-dollar home represents success. Maria, the waitress at a cafe I frequent, gave up hope of achieving success long ago.

If one tenth of the energy, which is spent by people erroneously chasing personal success, could be harnessed and redirected toward helping our fellow men, believe me, the world would take on a new and wonderful aspect immediately. If we all made living a good and helpful life our definition of success, Life would soon become wonderful for most everyone on the planet (including ourselves, of course).

It takes us back to the US or ME dichotomy, doesn't it? Where success is defined in terms of elevating and aggrandizing ME, the human condition will necessarily continue to deteriorate ("I do for me and not you."). Where success is defined in terms of US ("What positive things can we do for each other?") the human condition will, without question, begin improving immediately.

In a super competitive society, such ours - one where competition nears hallowed status and ranks up there with Baseball, Mom, and Apple Pie - we tend to belittle cooperation and relegate it to a less desirable position. Children are exposed to the competitive spirit from their very earliest experiences.

At the risk of being tarred and feathered and run out of town on a rail, I believe the relative importance of those two concepts (competition and cooperation) needs to be reversed. (I sense the rotten eggs targeting my front door!) People have to learn to cooperate, first, if mankind is going to survive in peace and comfort and good health. So long as we continue to instill in our children the belief that they have to be the best (that is, better than everybody else) there is little room in their lives to contemplate the necessity for, and usefulness of, cooperation.

Let me relate a short story. In the town where my wife and I raised our son there was a well-entrenched Little League type baseball program. Competition between teams, families, and fathers was absurdly intense - generation after generation. My son refused to be a part of it but loved to play. So, he and I started Saturday Morning Scramble Ball.

The rules were simple. The teams were always named Red and Blue. Everybody who showed up got to be out on the field every inning. (You haven't enjoyed baseball until you've seen four third basemen going after the ball at once.) Teams were determined by having the players blindly select a kernel of dried corn from a box - half red and half blue. Then, at the beginning of each new inning the teams were re-configured - again everybody drew a kernel to see which team he or she was on that inning. In the end, either the Red team or the Blue team usually had the most points (if anybody actually bothered to keep track). Since every player had been on each team, everybody 'won'. But the fun came in the playing and not in the winning. Well, everybody 'won' because everybody had a good time. Praise was universally issued for good plays, nice tries, hilarious antics, and general helpfulness. On Saturday mornings, our little ball pasture became the endorphin* center of the universe. (*Brain chemicals that produce happy feelings)

The point is, we played strictly for fun. The kids cooperated and shared and supported and uplifted each other. Any fan who began taking things too seriously was approached by a small, self-appointed, delegation of players and asked to get on board or leave. The only real problem we ever encountered, occurred at the point when so many youngsters defected from regular league play to scramble play that several of the more gung-ho parents threatened to string me up. (For better or worse, they didn't!)

Believe me, I'm not condemning Little League or even friendly competition in general. But the argument is just too often made that youngsters have to learn how to compete to be a success in life. See how shallow that argument seems when you configure Success and Happiness as has been done here. It is not competitive skill that makes one a success in life or on the job. It is knowledge of the task, good work habits, positive life goals, and a helpful bent on living. It doesn't take a competitive upbringing to foster those positive traits. Any thoughtful home can raise cooperative, responsible, forward looking, loving youngsters who are well prepared to 'succeed' in life and in the world of work.

Don't even try to suggest that without competition the great advances in science would never be made. People who believe their 'calling' in life is to improve the lot of their fellow men are naturally cooperative and their motivation is therefore far away from bonuses, promotions, fame and fortune. Those who argue the point, clearly have no conception of the truly necessary steps for saving mankind and improving its lot.

So, now that you are ready to look beyond stuff, money, fame, and winning as sources for Deep Down Forever Happiness, we will – in the next chapter - move on to the creation of your positive personal and social philosophy for living.

EXERCISE:
By now you are becoming a pro at relaxing and have found an abundance of positive behaviors that you've been exhibiting. In fact, by merely keeping track of them you undoubted found yourself being even more positive than usual. (That's okay, by the way!!) During the next twenty-four hours keep track of the things you do that are not so positive. Let's try and define that a bit more tightly.

You may think you're helping by bawling somebody out. It doesn't count as positive. The more typical negative events include things such as being rude, sarcastic, practical 'jokes', name calling, gossiping, arguing with an attitude, putting others down, any unkind or hurtful remark or innuendo, ignoring those who need attention, losing patience, indicating someone is below you or somehow less worthy, yelling at your family members (or neighbors or co-workers), and so on. You need to be honest with yourself, of course, or the exercise will bring you more harm than good.

CHAPTER FOUR
SECRET 2
Develop, Understand, and Practice a
Positive Philosophy for Living.

Positive, by both formal definition and common sense, refers to the opposite of Negative. Interestingly, I think, it is the negative side of life that often attracts people's attention first. Just watch the evening news - disasters, crimes, economic gloom and doom, war, poverty, disease. Almost as an afterthought some newscasts add a token, positive, item - usually at the end. Attempts at airing 'Good Stuff" newscasts have failed miserably. One would think people must have a driving need to hear about the negative side of life.

That is, in fact, a reasonable conclusion, considering the prime job of our Deep Mind is to keep us safe. In order to remain safe we have to know what negative (potentially hurtful) forces are out there needing to be avoided. The allure of the negative is part of our most basic built-in survival mechanism. Because of that, we have to specifically work at being positive beings. It is a conscious faculty - capacity - that humans, above all other animals, possess, but we must choose to utilize it. Where other animals can't make that choice, human beings can (and if they don't they are merely living like ....).

Let me try it one more time. Holding to a positive philosophy is not one of our most basic traits. In a sense, we have to rise above the more primitive needs and stances that are built into us. We can do that.   No other being in the entire known universe can do that!   I hope that makes you feel VERY special.

What are those more basic primitive needs? First, is self-protection - survival. It includes meeting our needs for safety, shelter, food, and (particularly in males) sexual activity. (Without that basic, high level, drive, the species would have died off young, so nothing that comes later, here, would matter.)

Just above that first-line level is our need to accomplish those most basic things with some degree of regularity and comfort and pleasure. It can be characterized as our need for positive consistency. Once free to explore our needs at that level, social interaction for reasons other than protection and survival begins to blossom. It is not until we are free to explore this level of existence that the possibility for positive approaches to living (interacting) can emerge.

An orphaned street kid in Brazil who struggles with survival every minute of every day is hardly going to have time or interest in creating and projecting a positive social philosophy. The same goes for millions and millions of people living sick and in poverty in the poorest developing countries (and in the slums of most every city in my own country). In situations of kill or be killed, take or starve, talking about how to become and stay Deep Down Forever Happy is not only irrelevant it is fully unbelievable as a concept.

Still, among the wealthy, the healthy, the intelligent, and the famous, Happiness is, far too often, also an elusive state of mind. It is essential to recognize and accept the big idea in that previous sentence.   Look at it again.   Does it say Happiness is a state of having lots of cool stuff? Lots of money? Lots of fame or status or power? No. It says Happiness is one hundred percent a state of mind. This immediately separates Happiness from all categories of stuff. It also separates Happiness from how other people think about you (much more in chapter six).

If I can't count on stuff or power or riches or fame or approval (and so on) to make and keep me Deep Down Forever Happy, what's left?

Think of all those things Happiness is not dependent on as the Exterior Factors. It then becomes easier to see what you have left to work with - the Interior Factors. Interior Factors are primarily thoughts and emotions. Thoughts can be broken down into several areas. One of those is Beliefs or Values. We all operate according to a set of beliefs and values whether we can state what they are or not. (Your Deep Mind knows!) Anybody who knows us can probably make a list of six to twelve observations that quite accurately define our system of Beliefs and Values because (remember) our behaviors are based on them.

As an example, let's take a look at two lists of regularly displayed behaviors that I jotted down about two of my 'acquaintances'. I'll call them Pete and Jake.

My list about Pete:

Expressed anger toward the bell ringer at the Christmas Kettle because he was in the way.

Took the last "Pudgy Pooch" toy from another person's shopping cart when she wasn't looking.

Called the new teen-boy worker at the fast food store an idiot for making a mistake on his order.

Kept his seat on the overloaded bus letting the old lady stand in the aisle beside him.

Spoke angrily at the waitress who allowed his coffee cup to get empty.

Kept the ten-dollar bill he received in change when it should have been a five.

My list about Jake:

Passed the bell ringer and, having previously made his contribution, said, (Not the boastful or face saving, "I've already given," but) "I appreciate your hard work and the time you give to help with this project."

Spoke to a waitress after his coffee cup had been empty for a few moments. "Looks like you timed that perfectly. Thank you."

Spoke to the embarrassed, newly blue vested, teenager who made a mistake as he checked Jake out at the hardware store. "Hey, we've all been new on the job at some point in our lives. Don't worry about it. I remember how it was."

Walked four blocks back to the ticket booth at the concert center to return the third ticket he had been given in error when he paid for only two.

Took time to speak with the fully ignored five-year-old brother of the new baby who was getting all the attention in her stroller at the store. "Your new little sister is really lucky to have a strong, big brother like you, I'll tell you that! Someday she'll understand how great that is, won't she?"

Okay. So, I made up Pete and Jake. But I'm sure a person of your intelligence gets the point. (I could have said, "But I'm sure you're really not so dumb as to miss my point." Which phrasing makes you feel better? Interestingly, it makes me - the speaker - feel better as well!).

Characterize Pete's philosophy of living in a word or short phrase. Negative. Disruptive. Humiliating. Insensitive. Unpleasant. Tactless. And most certainly, ME centered. What about Jake? Positive. Builds folks up. Compassionate. Uplifting. Helpful. US centered.

An obvious, basic, difference in the two approaches is where the comfort is aimed - Me or Us (My comfort comes first and yours certainly doesn't count vs. let's try and make it comfortable for both of us).

Ask a person how he feels right after he has verbally abused somebody else. If he is honest, he will say "Mad," or "Angry." Do the same after somebody has offered a kind word and you will hear just the opposite - good, happy, fine. The emotion attached to what we say lingers inside us longer than one might think. When it lingers as happiness, we learn about being happy (maybe even, Happy!). When it lingers as anger, we attach that emotion to our life in general and those in it. (Remember. Your Deep Mind is always listening to learn about you and what you want. It is interesting that angry responses are often motivated by the idea we will feel better after we "Tell it like it is" or "Tell him off," or "Get it off my chest". We usually don't. He feels worse. We feel worse, or at least no better. Those who had to witness the tirade feel worse and embarrassed that a fellow member of their species would act that way.)

The antiquated therapeutic approach of venting and rehashing our bad feelings over and over again is really NOT helpful. It has been a well-established, scientifically researched, psychological truth for more than fifty years that, in fact, the result is just the opposite - harmful. In most cases the more we talk about bad feelings the more time we spend feeling (reliving) bad, so the more conditioned we become to feeling bad and looking for and remembering the bad stuff in life. In most cases, bad or angry feelings don't really get 'locked up' somewhere deep inside us so they build up and eventually have to explode. They may be sitting in the Deep Mind as inappropriate directives that surface from time to time, but it is relatively easy to get rid of them using the technique I'll show you later on. And it's free.

The point: You are, therefore, no longer allowed to use the expression of anger in the name of being a therapeutic process. From now on that will be considered just a lame excuse to justify your bad behavior. When one doesn't know the easy alternative, I will teach you, an occasional outburst can, perhaps, be accepted - understood, at least. But once that element of ignorance has passed (new knowledge received), there is no excuse for it. If you believe you really feel better after you express anger at somebody, there is still work for you to do. Fortunately, there is that fairly simple solution.

With all that as background material, let's move on and examine the crux of a Positive Philosophy of living. A philosophy is, remember, an Interior activity - thoughts, beliefs, values. Notice I use the phrase Philosophy of living rather than Philosophy of life. Living implies action - what we do with our life. Life is mostly just not being dead - hardly a potential force for good in the world all by itself.

A Positive Personal and Social Philosophy follows from one or both of two basic assumptions without which none of this really matters because we would soon destroy our species and give the planet back to the cockroaches.

Basic Assumption One: The human species should

survive long after I'm gone, it should improve, and it should do so in planet-wide peace, comfort, and Happiness. (The view based on Altruism)

Basic Assumption Two: Even if you could care less about Assumption One (the long-term survival and well-being of the human species) can you accept this: When those about me are happy, content, healthy, and financially able to meet their own needs, they will be easier to live among and therefore my life will be much easier, safer, and generally more pleasant. It is therefore in my best interest to help improve the human condition. (The view based on Selfism - my term.)

Interestingly, both of the above basic assumptions require the same kinds of positive behaviors. Positive behaviors flow most easily from a positive philosophy.

Let me suggest four basic approaches philosophies of living may take. You undoubtedly have met some folks who illustrate each one.

Positive philosophies are love based and typically tell us what to do, usually to improve things for all concerned.

Negative philosophies may or may not be love-based, but typically tell us what not to do, often leaving one adrift and uncertain about what he is to do.

Hate based philosophies instruct us to inflict harm or death on others - usually some specified group.

There are also Isolationist Philosophies which require one to remain separated from others who believe differently, usually so one's set of beliefs cannot be compared side by side with others (challenged), thereby allowing no temptation to change (or grow?). Sometimes it is based on ideas of religious or racial purity.

So, your positive philosophy will direct your behaviors to help you provide the best that you can do for all of us. It may help for us to compare some of the behaviors typically flowing from it with some of those from negative or hate-based philosophies.

Love rather than hate
Help rather than hinder
Heal rather than kill or ignore

Live in peace rather than in war (or any kind of hurtful aggression)

Cooperate rather than compete

Suggest what to do rather than what not to do.

Build up rather than put down or 'put in his place'.

Govern inclusively rather than Brandishing power or excluding.

Compliment rather than disparage.

Listen rather than ignore or continually espouse.

Discuss rather than argue.

Search for answers rather than blame (lots more about this later).

Retrain rather than punish.

Plan rather than worry.

Engage positively rather than torment.

Enjoy your own foibles rather than being embarrassed at them or worrying about them as being signs of personal weakness.

Be patient rather than becoming irritated (unless, of course, you have never made a mistake or dawdled, yourself☺).

Accept new ideas as food for thought rather than as objects to be ridiculed in ignorance or rejected outright.

Accept yourself rather than reject yourself (If there are things you don't like about you, make plans to gradually change them into things you will like, when that is possible.)

Allow others the right to espouse (explain or advocate), if not act on, their own beliefs rather than throttling them. (Who knows what insight you might experience or what philosophic bit you might have the chance to pass on for the others to consider.)

Allow for the possibility that you may be wrong on some issue or belief rather than holding the absolutist position, "I am without any doubt absolutely right on this." (Gather data and interpret it honestly. That's what our human brain does best.)

The bottom line is this. A Positive Philosophy cares for and builds other people up, realistically, honestly, and compassionately, just because it is the right thing to do. (Not because it provides you with some personal gain like buying friendship, status, or acceptance or works to relieve your guilt.) If this is how you live your life you are well on your way to Deep Down Forever Happiness.

If it seems difficult for you to formulate a Positive Philosophy of Life, look into the book mentioned before - The Secrets of Deep Mind Mastery. It outlines one such approach in great detail. You may find it can be a useful starting point. To make family life positive consult books such as, The One Rule Plan for Family Happiness and Trouble Proofing Kids. [See Book List at end of this manual.]

CHAPTER FIVE
SECRET 3
Living a Life of Integrity

We've all done it - said something harsh or unpleasant and then wished we could take it back - rewind time and start over would really be our wish. Why do we typically get that after the fact, uneasy, feeling? We certainly seemed to mean the comment at the moment it was delivered.

There are a number of possible reasons. Most likely it just didn't represent how we really wanted to act so we want to retract it. If, deep inside, we believe that our interactions with others should be designed to build rather than destroy, unkind words are virtually always out of place and we know that.

There may be one part of us that feels it is important and acceptable to assert our rights to always be treated perfectly by others, while another part of us believes we should interact with others on the basis of understanding, patience, and/or compassion. That sets up a competition of a sort, doesn't it? Both ways can't be right - both accompanying feelings can't be right.

In the least, most of us are feeling a tinge of guilt for that instance of imposing bad, hurtful, feelings rather than spreading good feelings.

That wish to retract could also be motivated by a straightforward, unadulterated need to be a good 'businessman' and never offend for fear the other party will stop 'buying' - acting positively toward us. We are bothered by the prospect that the remark may cause that to happen.

For some, that desire to retract hurtful remarks stems

from an issue of image. It may tarnish the image one has of himself. It may cause him to wonder what kind of a person he really is deep down inside. For others, it is a matter of the image others will have of him because of it. They will think less of him. They may think of him as a bad person. They may decide to avoid him so as to not risk being hurt by him again.

After such an event, do you find yourself apologizing, feeling guilty, or finding some excuse for your behavior? Apologies are generally accepted forms of social behavior even though they can never undue what was said or done. Because of that - apology aside - the other person will never really view you in the same way as he did before. Sometimes apologies may be truly sincere. Sometimes they are merely a matter of going through the expected social graces.

Apologizing often becomes separated from any genuine feeling of remorse. That may be largely due to the way children are typically introduced to the concept of apologizing. They mistreat another person in some way. A parent or teacher says to them, "Now you apologize at once. Tell him you're sorry." The child, who is probably in no way really sorry, still goes through the disingenuous process of the apology. What does he learn? That you may be able to buy yourself out of serious trouble by lying about your true feelings. In fact, your parents seem to insist on it so it must be okay to lie that way!

Once a person begins feeling guilty for something he has said or done, most folks have no useful way to relieve themselves of it. They may try to 'make it up' to the aggrieved person but that's really just a way of buying your way back into somebody's good graces. Think of guilt as a force or message arising from the Deep Mind when your action is incompatible with how it believes you have previously told it you wanted to behave (in the majority of cases).

When one finds himself in constant need of excusing himself for his behavior there is bound to be a major problem - a major disparity between the underlying philosophy (intentions) and typical behavior. Sometimes that relates to having directives that were set into place in your Deep Mind by others - parents, clergy, siblings, perhaps. They are not really yours or the variety you want, but they are still there directing your life (or at least pestering you unmercifully about the way you are living your life).

Perhaps the most popular excuse for inappropriate, rude, and hurtful words and behavior is to lay it on your 'temper' as if *temper* were a 'thing' somewhere that had a mind of its own - a mind that is always more powerful than yours. RUBBISH! Temper is a descriptive term which refers to uncontrolled, hurtful, outbursts. Stop thinking of it as a noun (a thing) and begin recognizing that it is a verb (an action - your action).

In a tiny percent of cases, temper outbursts are reflective of a physical malfunction in the brain. Medical treatment should be sought for such constant, regular, uncontrollable, outbursts. In all other cases take steps to control it and then eliminate it. (More later.)

In most cases, temper outbursts are tied directly to the Deep Mind's prime directive - protect and preserve ME. When the Deep Mind has learned to characterize little things (such as put downs, challenges, affronts, rudeness) as being life threatening, you can bet there will be a huge and immediate reaction fully beyond the control of your conscious mind (the part you are aware of - thoughts, memories, plans, perceptions of the world around you, and so on.). Severing that inappropriate connection is essential and you will be taught an approach for doing that later.

How do such hurtful connections get made? Probably through the process of conditioning. It occurs when two things occur together, or one follows right after the other as if being caused by the first. In an extreme example, if a parent calls the child an idiot and then beats him you can bet the idea of being called an idiot is getting quite fully connected to the pain that follows. In other words, "Idiot" comes to equal a threat to that child's wellbeing - survival. The Deep Mind has no option other than to rage and try to destroy the source. So, later on, when someone else calls him an idiot, what kind of behavior can be expected?

The solution is to sever the tie between those things

that trigger rage and the Deep Mind's interpretation that they are life threatening. The 'life threat' does not have to be physical violence. It can be threatening words or deeds that fall short of violence. The withdrawal of love is one such instance.

"You're just no good," followed by isolation in a dark, cold room as punishment. A disgruntled, "I just can't understand you," followed by a period of being ignored or clearly rejected. "You're just not a man," followed by his father's turned back and additional words of derision.

When those associations appear to threaten one's basic lovability or worth (existence) you can bet those phrases or ones similar in meaning spoken by others later on WILL trigger life protecting outbursts.

If you react with a "temper" fix the misguided process, don't use it as an excuse for your bad behavior. (Later.)

Let me briefly discuss one other frequent reason behind unpleasant - not positive, destructive - comments directed at others. In a word, it is modeling. When a child grows up in an environment or with a parent or influential sibling that exhibits short fused, rude, destructive, verbal reactions to others, the child learns to react in that way as well. It seems right and appropriate because that's how the important person (people) in his life react.

There is no such thing as "Do as I say, not as I do." Kids (and Deep Minds) believe actions over words or admonishments every time. Here is a not so elegant illustration of unrecognized modeling that came from a counseling session I was having with a family. At one emotionally charged point the father turned to his son and said: "How many dammed times have I told you to stop cussing?" Everybody in the room saw the problem except the father.

Back to the more immediate topic of this chapter. How do we come to wish our comment could be retracted? What allows such missteps to take place in the first place?

If you find yourself really wanting to know, one thing seems clear. There is at least the glimmer (if not much, much, more) of a positive philosophy of living lurking around inside you. Clearly, you acted in a way you later really wish you hadn't. Each such behavior that is contrary to how we want to act represents one or more Deep Mind directives we need to get rid of. When the Deep Mind really isn't sure how you want it to react in a given situation it just randomly selects a directive from the general category and causes you to act on it. (Reaction to a teacher, to failure, success, fear, etc.) Even when it does have a good idea about your basic wishes, it may select a less appropriate one just because it's there, 'close by' the others. That may be due to the Deep Mind's notorious carelessness or it may reflect a degree of generalized tension or just poor Deep Mind housekeeping on your part. (More later)

When we (or our Deep Mind) are living under great stress and tension, we tend to make less adequate - less precise - choices of words and behaviors. Again, that is not an excuse for bad behavior. It is a reason - a reason that should suggest to us that we need to take steps to fix it. When we don't have the knowledge about how to fix such things, we just remain there feeling helpless. Tension rises even more, and things get worse - certainly our degree of happiness decreases.

How does such mental and emotional tension come about? In several ways. Sometimes just through exhaustion - a state when no human process functions efficiently. More typically it arises when it is not immediately obvious what the right solution or answer to a problem should be. We remain torn between two or more possibilities or torn about by the emptiness of no possibilities. That may happen because there really is no best answer (Do I use what money I have to buy my child's medicine or buy him food?). Or, it may happen because one tends to stop at the level of worrying rather than moving on to making plans (see a later chapter). Worriers live in a constant state of unnecessary tension.

The Deep Mind is a solution generating dynamo. It loves problems and questions. In fact, it reacts poorly when given directions, reacts even more poorly when given commands, and usually refuses to even consider negative information ('Don't do this or that.' In fact, it typically ignores the negative - don't - and treats it as if it were positive. How, then, might it interpret the direction, "Don't use drugs?"). Later on, you will learn how to phrase your communications with your Deep Mind in terms of short, clear, positive questions. I'll just add here that approaching a child with words is essentially approaching his Deep Mind so what works best for that works best for the child.

Let me switch gears briefly. What if a person really doesn't feel bad after reading somebody the riot act or after verbalizing some other destructive message in somebody's direction? What if a person feels fully justified about treating others badly? It most likely means that person really doesn't intend to live by a positive philosophy and gives little thought to his role and responsibility in the comfortable survival of mankind. It probably means he lives a very Me centered - selfish - life. Because of those things his actions match his philosophy so there is no tension - no reason to retract any of the destructive things he says. In other words, since there is no underlying positive philosophy to match with his behaviors, destructive words produce no tension - they do not represent a mismatch to his philosophy. (They may very likely cause him to become socially isolated by others or the legal system, however.)

If you have the personality described as socially destructive (just above), but if you also accept the premise of the previous chapter (When the people around you continue to be unhappy, violent, poor, and/or ill they will tend to make your life uncomfortable and expensive), and if you cherish your own safety and comfort, it still only makes logical sense for you to try and make some positive changes in the way you go about living your life relative to others.

You have at least three choices. (1) Continue to live in discomfort and perhaps fear, shelling out extra tax money to support the homeless, house the criminals, and treat the mentally ill. (2) Move to a place where everybody is perfect and self-sufficient like you are. Or, (3) Help fix the social problems that are causing your discomfort.

Living among happy, comfortable, well cared for people provides a happy, comfortable, and usually safe, community (family) in which to live.   List the things about those around you that bother (discomfort) you the most.   Beside each of your entries, list ways to help that person fix his problem. Then, decide how you can be a useful part of that process. (Sometimes we find it is we who have the problem!)

Beginning by being 'nice' to others will go just about as far as anything and takes no dollars out your pocket and no time off your calendar. If you characterize yourself as being impatient (again, a reason, not an excuse, for hurtful behavior) here are some things you might try in order to reduce that reaction.

Live according to a more effective - flexible - time schedule; one in which you allow time for the little problems and inconveniences that are bound to come your way throughout most days. If you weren't so cramped for time those aggravations might not really seem aggravating at all.

Spend time thinking about your outlook on life - your perspective. I offer you a piece of mine. It defuses and nullifies the annoying aspects of just about every little inconvenience or petty problem that comes my way. When a waitress brings me green beans rather than baked beans, or a car splashes me as I walk home after a rain, or my hat is blown to Timbuktu never to be recovered, or there is something wrong with my order from the drive through, I say to myself, "If that's the worst that happens to me today, my life is in really great shape."

Finally, recognize and accept this well-established adage about human behavior. "At any given moment, a person behaves the only way he can behave given all the forces impinging on him. If he could act otherwise, he would have to."

Examine that in light of one of your own less than stellar responses to somebody. You did or said what you did because it seemed like the thing you had to do or say at that moment. If you had some additional piece of information that would have changed your perspective, you would have been influenced by it and behaved differently. You would have reacted the only way you could have at that moment - given what you knew and felt.

In summary, this secret to Deep Down Forever Happiness is to live a life which, as closely as possible, reflects your underlying positive philosophy of life. The degree to which you vary from that, represents how far you are away from Happiness. The greater the disparity, the greater the tension, and the less the Happiness.

So, understand the positive philosophy of living that guides you, and establish a set of behaviors that match it as closely as possible.

EXERCISE

Review your list of the good things you do – things you do that you approve of – things that tend to make the world a better place one small act at a time. Use it as a basis for writing the positive philosophy that appears to be guiding you. Begin by just rewording what you did into a rule you seem to be following. Let's try some examples.

On your list, you may find entries such as these:

I smiled at strangers as I passed them.

I nodded and said hi to people on the elevator.

I said good morning to everybody at work as I passed their desk this morning.

I answered the phone with a cheery tone and greeting.

Think about a short, positive, Directive you want to deposit in your Deep Mind – one that is all inclusive of things like those on your list. One possibility would be, I greet people positively. That directive, or one similar to it, is a wonderful starting place. It is easy to act on. Watch the reactions you get from people. Think back through them at night. What kind of feeling overtakes you as you see those sober faces break into smiles; as you hear happy words returned from previously silent mouths; and as you see those folks begin passing on your positive behavior to others? (Take time to answer the question.)

It is an easy match to make. It is, therefore, an easy source for immediate Happiness.

CHAPTER SIX
SECRET 4
You Only Really Ever Need Your Own Approval

One of the pluses about living a life based on positive integrity is that, in order to be Happy, you can pretty much just forget about what other people think or say about you. When you behave according to your positive philosophy, THAT match becomes your proof of self-worth. It immediately removes the necessity to live up to the standards others try to impose on you. Most social pressure evaporates because it doesn't exist for you. Social pressure requires two things. First, some 'required' aspect of social acceptability that was set by others, which you don't (or don't want to) reach. Second, somebody else telling you that you should or have to reach it. Disregard either the other person's goal or the false authority of the other person and the felt pressure is gone.

When you lay in bed at night, you have but one question to ask and answer: "Today, how well did I live up to my beliefs about being a good and useful human being?" (Your positive philosophy.) You never have to toss and turn about whether you lived up to your parents' expectations, or your friend's expectations, or your neighbors' expectations, or . . . Your self-worth is not dependent upon being accepted or approved of by anybody other than you. If your life doesn't live up to their expectations, that has to be left as their problem, not yours. Their business is NOT setting your expectations for yourself.

Does this mean you can reject all social expectations - all social do's and don'ts, rights and wrongs? Maybe. Maybe not. It's hard to fault a nice guy even when he may behave a bit out of the box. If you are guiding yourself by a positive social philosophy your behavior WILL be generally acceptable, even if not specifically acceptable.

For example: "He's a nice guy alright but his hair is way too long." (Someone else's expectation or rule about your hair length.) "She's a dear, kind, person, but she wears the same half dozen outfits over and over and over again." (Someone else's expectation about your wardrobe.) "They are a really nice family, but you'd think they could afford a better house and car." (Probably meaning they believe you should be striving for a better house and car the way they do.)

When your purpose - goal - is to live a life of positive integrity, things such as hair length, number of outfits in your closet, or the size or quality of house and car just don't enter the Happiness equation. "I'm Happy for being the person I am, not for the stuff I have, or my appearance, or how others judge my financial situation. I can't be put down for how I am because how I am is how I aim to be."

If you do reject or defy certain social standards (hair length, for example) you have to understand there will be those out there who will try to put you down, ridicule you, even reject you because you don't meet the expectations they have set for you. Sometimes that occurs because they truly believe their way of life (a way measured in terms of stuff, power, and prestige) is the only, true, right, way. Since you aren't living that way there has to be something 'wrong' with you. Such judgments often arise as a self-centered, self-protective, face-saving, device. "If I would allow (or accept) that other way of life, then the validity of my way would have to come into question."

You may run up against situations in which you have to choose between your way and their way. In the workplace, for example, there may be rules or expectations about dress and grooming that you are required to meet. Shoes and socks, perhaps. Combed hair. Shirt and tie. Shaved face. You get the idea. If those things are not on your list of important aspects of life then you have to choose - giving in to a few seemingly less important requirements - or the job. If your job requires that you appear in a certain way or else be rejected by your clients or customers (or boss) you have to make a choice between those aspects of appearance and the job.

The bottom line is that if you find it necessary to make some small adjustments in order to get a job, it is unlikely it will affect your feeling of self-worth or your integrity. When we live among people who don't believe in some of the elements dictated by our Positive Philosophy, we often have to give in a little in order to feed our family. That will be far higher on your list of important beliefs than not wearing a tie or not allowing your hair to grow. Lying about a product for your boss, however, may cross the line and you will need to refuse or look elsewhere for employment.

As you assemble your 'list' of positive characteristics and beliefs that make up your positive philosophy of living, you will want to begin clumping them into a least two, general, categories. The highest group will be those beliefs you will not abandon - being helpful; being non-violent except in life-threatening situations; treating others with respect; etc, whatever yours might be. The other group will be those that have some situational element in them - shoes or tie or suit at work when, to you, being dressed that way should not be a measure of your worth as a person; speeding in your car, when an emergency requires it, even though you believe speeding is potentially devastating to yourself and others; telling a fib when it saves face for somebody else but does not affect anyone in a truly hurtful manner, even though being truthful is high on your 'good behavior' list; and so on.

How can such a second list even exist when integrity requires absolute, unwavering, values and beliefs? If that second list were labeled, "Behaviors I can change whenever it suits my fancy," then it would not be a set of beliefs at all, would it. It would be more a list of things to maybe, possibly, consider from time to time, perhaps. Think of it as being labeled, "Behaviors I can fudge a bit when there is a greater social good to be accomplished." You are saying that in most instances my stated belief seems to serve mankind and me best, although there are reasonable exceptions in the service of necessary comfort, safety, and happiness. Some beliefs are virtually invariable. Some are not. Thus, the two lists.

A brief Review: Deep Down Forever Happiness depends on maintaining a match between your behavior and your own positive belief system. That frees you from pressures being exerted from others to behave in the way they think you should. Some of your most important values are invariable. A few others may be modified briefly when the social situation suggests that will be for some greater good.

When we fall asleep at night, we want to be able to say, "I lived my life today the way I want to live my life every day." Sometimes we may not be able to say that - well, not entirely, at least. In those instances, we take note of the problem area (value or behavior) and pledge to work on it the next day. It is not a worry because you will have a plan readily available to use in making such changes (later). We have faith in our ability.

Frequently, people find that even though they are generally able to keep to their philosophy there are still certain people (or kinds of people) with whom problems often seem to arise. Rather than asking, "What's wrong with those people?" ask, "What is there about me that won't let me deal appropriately (positively) with them?"

See how that changes your approach immediately. So long as you make it his problem there may be nothing you can do about your behavior - reaction. But, once you make it your problem, you can begin to fix it at once.

Let's face it, some people are very difficult to get along with and, sadly, that presents a huge problem for them. But it is your ability to get along with them that is YOUR concern. Often just avoiding them helps solve the problem (but that doesn't help you grow). Deciding not to argue with even their most offensive or outlandish positions can help. Not encouraging conversation on his "hot button" topics often avoids the issue. Instead of allowing his behavior to make you angry at him, re-characterize the situation and feel compassion for him because he has developed some universally irritating quality. It is, remember, HIS right to set his expectations about his own behavior. What we demand for ourselves, we must allow others!

If your purpose is to change his mind (allow him to explore alternative beliefs and behaviors), different approaches are necessary, of course. Remember, in an argument, both positions tend to become solidified rather than either actually changing. Arguing, lecturing, and offering un-requested advice, are the least effective methods for changing someone's mind, beliefs, or behavior. (Please read that sentence again.)

Successfully modeling a more appropriate way of life is the most effective approach. (It requires patience and long term commitment.) Pleasantly asking for clarification of, or the reasons behind, certain statements or positions is always better than confronting a person about the error or worthlessness of his beliefs. Listen to the answer (if it is offered) without comment. ("I'm interested in hearing how you came to that conclusion.") Any comment that hints at disagreement has the potential for turning the exchange into an argument (and arguments, remember, serve no useful purpose). There are times and places to confront disagreements but pick your battles very carefully.

Once a person hears himself explaining or defining an inappropriate, illogical, or otherwise hurtful position, he will often begin doing the appropriate thinking about it (remodeling it) on his own. That seldom happens if he is immediately forced to defend it. Defending one's belief automatically strengthens it. Cults and most religions use this basic human characteristic to create steadfast followers. In fact, studies show the more pain (broadly defined) one has to endure to defend a belief or way of life, the more deeply entrenched it becomes. Most extreme initiation activities are born out of that fact. Those who survive the most severe rites become the staunchest believers. Consider Fraternity loyalty as one example and the beatings required for gang membership as another.

So, why this foray into behavior modification of others when my position is that all one has to do is be true to himself and that others should be allowed to do the same? Remember, that one of the reasons for keeping others happy, secure, healthy, and so on, is to maintain your own all-round comfort in your social setting. When others live according to a positive philosophy, your life and all the lives they touch will go better (not to mention their own). So, when you can help others see and feel the tremendous advantage that comes with living a positive, integrity-based, life (or even just a non-hurtful way of life), you've made a convert and the world becomes just that much more friendly and supportive – comfortably helpful.

If you truly believe living a life of integrity is the best way to go about living, then somewhere on your list of positive traits is going to be an entry about helping others come to realize that a world populated by folks with positive agendas improves things for all of us. (Model! Model! Model!)

Make the items on your list as broad as possible without becoming meaningless. For example, instead of a list containing all these entries (bathe every morning, brush teeth after every meal, wear clean clothes, groom hair, use deodorant, etc.) use a single more inclusive, obviously meaningful term such as, 'I Want to Maintain Good Personal Hygiene'.

Beginning each item on your positive behavior list with the phrase, "I want to . . ." personalizes and empowers the entry. It stipulates the approved behavior. It gives it your immediate endorsement. The Deep Mind appreciates such a clear, straight forward, no beating around the bush, approach. You are saying, "Here it is as simply put as I can positively state it."

By stating each entry as a positive behavior that you want to express and maintain also makes it easy to evaluate. You either did it or you didn't. Let's look at a few examples.

I want to greet people in positive ways.
I want to act in helpful ways.
I want to tell the truth.
I want to be polite.
I want to resist making hurtful remarks.
I want to build people up even if only in small ways.

I want to listen (more than tell or argue).

I want to present myself as a comfortable person for others to be near.

I want to do my reasonable share at work.

I want to make sure that what I have to say is really of interest or use to those I'm telling.

I want to make time for my family (perhaps be even more person-specific - husband, mother, children, teacher, associate, others).

You only ever really need your own approval to find Deep Down Happiness. Approval is a positive evaluation of your success level. Success is defined as living up to the positive values (exhibiting the behaviors) you want to exhibit. The only approval rating you ever need for Happiness (success) is your own approval. The rating system is pretty simple. Ask: How well am I living up to my positive philosophy of living?

All you need in order to feel fully successful is to know that you are living up to (or closely approaching) your own positive standards. Let's look at that again. All you need in order to feel fully successful is to know that you are living up to your own positive standards.

Do you need new cars to feel successful? Do you need a big house or a weekend home or boat to feel successful? Do you need a beautiful or handsome spouse to feel successful? Do you need a large income to feel successful? Do you need power, stuff, or prestige, to feel successful?

If success requires none of those things, than what do you need? (Fill in the blank!) All I need to feel fully successful is _____ (peak back two paragraphs if you need to).

EXERCISE:

Restate the list of positive traits you want to be exhibiting. Use the format suggested in this chapter. I want to _____. You may have found some ideas in this and the previous chapters that you want to add to your list. You may want to collapse several entries into just one more encompassing behavioral statement. You may even decide to expand or eliminate some. You may want to begin categorizing your list into segments - At Home, At Work, In Public, At Play. (If that doesn't seem like it would be helpful, forget it.)

CHAPTER SEVEN
SECRET 5
Altruism Must Replace Selfism

A quick glance into the dictionary tells us that the definition for Altruism is the unselfish regard for or devotion to others. A similar quick glance won't provide a definition for Selfism because I made up the term. I intend it to represent behavior that is one of the opposites of altruism. One opposite could be the destructive disregard of others' rights and feelings. That is not exactly what I intend.

Selfism encompasses all those behaviors that put ME first and OTHERS second (or 55th). It could more rightly be defined as the state in which one puts himself first and others less than first. Let's begin exploring this concept by listing some examples of Selfism.

I am going to spend money on that new outfit (even though I don't need it and I know there are kids having to go to bed hungry at night right here in my town).

I am going to spend my time out on my boat on Saturday (even though I know my child's all-school picnic needs volunteers).

I am going to buy a five hundred-thousand-dollar house (even though there are a hundred, homeless people in my community who need shelter).

I am going to spend fifty thousand dollars on a new car I don't need (even though there are dozens of single mothers in my community who can't take good jobs across town because they have no affordable way to get to them).

I am going to spend twenty-five thousand dollars on my son's 16th birthday bash (even though there are hundreds of sixteen-year olds in my city who can't afford school clothes, tutoring, school supplies, and medical treatment).

I am going to spend ___ thousands of dollars on my wedding so I can put on a lavish show, rather than using that money to help the needy or important research or literacy programs or ...

I am going to spend five thousand dollars on a vacation (when there are . . .).

You get the idea. I personally believe there are few sources for greater happiness than regularly helping those in need and supporting the positive future of mankind. And I don't mean just a little. I mean budget-bulging giving. It provides a deep down genuine, love based, reason for making money.

I know I'm the odd-ball - the odd-man-out - when it comes to such beliefs. I always have been. Many ask me, "Why work so hard making money if you're just going to give it away?" Or, "Why work so hard making money when you're not going to be able to use it for the stuff you want?" or, "Why work so hard making money if you're not going to stash it away for a comfortable retirement?"

What do you suppose I tell them? First of all, I usually don't even respond because it's my business, not theirs. Second, nobody has any business knowing how much I give away. Third, if they have to ask the question, they are clearly deeply steeped in their own Selfism. They will say: "I earned it so I get to spend it on myself." I don't argue with them. I feel sorry for them, but I don't argue the point. I feel sorry for all the folks they could be helping, but I don't argue with them. I feel bad that so long as they stick to such a philosophy, they will never be able to understand or experience true Deep Down Forever Happiness, but I don't argue with them.

Must one live in poverty to be Happy? That is not what I am intending to say. The fact that I choose to live at a substantially reduced financial level and have absolutely every 'thing' I could possibly envision wanting, does not mean I believe everybody should live my way. My way works wonderfully for me. My joy doesn't come from obtaining stuff or status or social acceptance. It comes from knowing I'm making a difference in people's lives. I'm sure I will give away many more copies of this book, for example, than will be sold. Nowhere in my list of positive goals will you find being rich or famous.

I no longer have family responsibilities the way I did as a younger man. Back then it was important for me to make sure the members of my family had their needs sufficiently met. Of course, since they shared my philosophy, they didn't have the gluttonous needs that many folks have. Even the dozens of foster children we cared for through the years soon settled comfortably into our lifestyle and with few exceptions went on to live lives successfully based on a Positive Social Philosophy of living. I'm particularly proud of that since most came to us as teenage boys from juvenile court.

Focus. Work hard to put stuff into perspective. We all need some stuff. None of us should rely on stuff as our means for seeking basic happiness. We can enjoy stuff, but we must not need stuff to make our life seem complete - Happy.

People often look at me over the tops of their glasses because of my conversation openers with young people. I suppose the more common, usual comments from folks reflect questions such as, "What do you want to be when you grow up," or "What sports are you into?" or "What's your favorite subject?"

My line is usually something like, "So, how have you and your family helped make the world a better place this week?"

The responses are fascinating. Parents are typically britches-wetting embarrassed at, and made uneasy by, the question. Teenagers shrug and probably think, "What a weirdo!" (I prefer eccentric, thank you!) Children are almost always thoughtful and give a reasonable answer. One answer typically reminds them of others. They almost always understand what kinds of things it takes to make the world a better place. At that point the parents relax - on the outside at least - and beam proudly, wondering, perhaps, where on earth their kid learned to be so perceptive.

I've found we can all take lessons from listening to children, especially those between the ages of eight and twelve. They know exactly what it takes to build a user-friendly world, perhaps because they so often find themselves on the short end of the stick. One has to wonder what happens to those generally astute insights as we grow older.

Selfism - I want stuff, and power, and good looks, and prestige, and money, and eventually better stuff than the neighbors, better looks, more prestige, and more money. (And I'm still not really Deep Down Forever Happy! Hmmm?)

Altruism - I'm going to put a twist on the typical definition, so it comes out this way: the unselfish regard for or devotion to others and oneself. What I'm trying to convey is that I am not more worthy of Happiness than anyone else AND no one else is more worthy of Happiness than I am. I want to shift it toward US rather than THEM. Mother Theresa may have had a strictly THEM orientation and that may be pure altruism - always putting others first - but not many folks are put together that way.

Let me offer my modified definition of Altruism: Doing as much as I can for those who are in need. (That includes me when I truly qualify.)

It suggests maintaining a balance between me (my needs) and them (their needs) and allows for individual differences. The phrase, "as much as I can," has to be individually defined. Some are capable of giving and doing more and spending more time helping than are others. For some that could mean 90% of their income or free time. Others will see it as being 10% or 5%. In my own experience and my experiences with thousands of others, the larger that percentage grows, the more Joy and Happiness one finds.

Again, it refers back to the specific set of positive principles (values, behaviors) one states in his or her Positive Philosophy. Smiles and nods and a quick "Hi, there!" cost nothing in money and typically nothing in extra time since you are probably on your way to or from anyway when such opportunities present themselves.

Altruism springs from a Positive Social and Personal Philosophy of living. Selfism does not. Selfism is supported by a generally uncaring philosophy, which acknowledges that I am the most important person in my world and therefore I will see to it that I (and perhaps my loved ones) are well taken care of. It seldom considers the needs or welfare of other people - outsiders. When it does, it often comes out like this: "I take care of myself and others should take care of themselves." Don't let the fully false logic in the statement fool you.

The statement falsely implies 'my hard work' and 'their laziness'. It really says: "I am among the fortunate that have been able to reach the place where I can take care of myself. Those who have had less opportunity or native ability or have had to endure more hardships should just take care of themselves as well."

Stated that way, the illogic shouts at us. So, do we help care for those who are truly in need or do we just say, "Tough luck. The forces of the Universe intend for you to suffer!", and ignore their plights?

I spoke of it earlier. One's philosophy of living is based in large part on how one views the importance of the human species. If one believes, as I do, that it is precious beyond any other life form in the known universe, then it becomes something to care for, and comfort, and improve and support in every possible way. No other being in the known universe has the capacity to love the way humans do. No other being can look to and plan for the future – one's own and that of his species and the planet on which it rides. No other species can contemplate its own eventual death thereby being uniquely able to understand the preciousness of life itself.

If, on the other hand, one's philosophy suggests no special regard for the human species beyond "ME" and what other people can do for "ME" in my here and now, then that philosophy cannot be positive in the sense I'm using the term. Such a philosophy allows one to ravage the planet, destroy the life supporting environment, obliterate portions of the human race that one doesn't approve of or sees as a threat to one's own self-centered ways, and to ignore the plights of millions of hopeless human beings both close to home and far away. A person with such a non-positive philosophy takes no steps to improve the planet or the general human condition now or for the future.

Few, if any of us, are totally guided by either just Altruism or just Selfism. We find ourselves somewhere on a gradient between the extremes of each. The extreme of Selfism might be characterized as the obliteration of all those who refuse or are unable to serve MY personal, self-centered, needs. The extreme of Altruism might be characterized as giving up all personal physical pleasures, possessions, and comforts so others can have what they need even if it kills me.

Let me add a short, illustrative, true story. (I think it's humorous!) I was once at a luncheon meeting where we were finalizing the campaign to convince voters to raise the tax which supported our County Mental Health Program. A waiter entered and got our attention. "The headlights are on in the red, limited edition, Thunderbird in the north parking lot." We looked around. The owner stood to go take care of the problem. It was a priest.

I'm not picking on priests. I'm illustrating the truth that we ALL live somewhere on that continuum between the two extremes. My goal is to live in such a way that my basic needs are met and that I feel comfortable and safe as near to the Altruism end of that scale as I can. The Hitlers of the world live at or near the other extreme.

My greatest personal concern is that during the past sixty years, it appears to me that more and more folks (I'm speaking of the developed countries) are approaching life on the Selfism half of that line and fewer and fewer folks are intentionally populating the Altruism half. Mankind cannot long survive with that current, Self-centered, configuration. The gap between the haves and the have nots is growing at an exponential rate and history shows that has always represented a conflagration in the making. I suppose this chapter represents my plea for you to help reverse that permanently destructive trend. (Think about school shootings, the rampant teen violence in our country, and the well-entrenched gang subculture if you need further justification for instilling Positive Social Philosophies in our children – and that requires unvarying, clear-cut, modeling.)

My greatest personal hope lies in the knowledge that there are proven methods for reversing that trend and that they can be used to build a world-wide union of people pledged to living and loving according to Positive Personal Philosophies that can span all religions and ethnic considerations. It will be accomplished one person at a time as each one of us works to build his or her own Positive Personal and Social Philosophy of living.

EXERCISE:

Draw a line across a sheet of paper. Label the left end Pure Selfism. Label the right end, Pure Altruism. Divide it in half by a short line at the center; then divide each of those two segments in half again so there are four segments. During the next few days or weeks study the gradient as you ask yourself what percent of the time you are living within each quarter of that continuum.

Maybe it will help to name each segment as you move from left right: very selfish, sort of selfish, sort of altruistic, very altruistic. It may also help to label each end with a word or phrase about the possibility for achieving Happiness at that extreme (altruism could be labeled "Great Deep Down Forever Happiness"; the Selfism end could be labeled "Happiness is always out of reach."

This is merely a device to help you begin sorting through the behaviors your philosophy seems to be dictating. It will be up to you, of course, to determine if you want to make any changes.

Each behavior that you consider and place somewhere along that line probably reflects a Deep Mind Directive. As they come up, place them on one of two lists: one made up of those you want to be sure to encourage within yourself, and another of those you really what to eliminate. Next to each behavior you want to eliminate jot down a behavior (directive) you'd like to exhibit instead - one that would rightfully sit on the opposite end of the continuum.

CHAPTER EIGHT
SECRET 6
Take Good Care of Yourself and Others

So, you want to find Deep Down Forever Happiness, and you are now working hard to plant yourself and your philosophy firmly somewhere along the Altruistic end of the Living Style Continuum presented in Chapter Seven. It may have appeared, back there, that I believe you have to live in a small, stone-walled cubical furnished with only a mattress on the floor, a candle for light, and a tin plate and cup from which to eat. Really, that is not my take on living a Deep Down Forever happy life. (You may also have a spoon! JOKE!)

Fun, happiness, pleasure are three important components in a well-rounded life. If by now you can't define Happiness as a close match between a positive social/personal philosophy and the behaviors you exhibit, I've not done an adequate job.

That leaves the roles and sources of fun and pleasure for us to discuss. I have characterized Happiness as a long-term state, which is settled in deep within a person's mind. Fun and pleasure are momentary states or events or experiences. There is nothing permanent about them. They come. They go. They provide positive feelings that last for a while and then fade and disappear.

It should be clear, then, how mistaking one for the other (fun and pleasure for Happiness) sets one up for major, long term, problems. Hoping not to muddy the waters further let me reintroduce the idea of happiness with the lower case 'h'. It will refer to our emotional reactions to fun and pleasure. I feel the need to use the term because it IS the term people have used for centuries to describe the feelings that stem from fun and pleasure. Those feelings, like fun and pleasure, are only momentary events. I can be happy while at the amusement park and later as I relive some of the highlights of the day, but that is not Forever Happy.

Perhaps I should have invented another term to represent what I mean by Happy. How about 'Zippyocity' or 'Perkitoria' or 'Plickistomy'? I think we're better off sticking with the capital 'H' since we already attach to that word the meaning that I intend. Integrity is a noun not a feeling, so it won't work at the emotional level. Saying we feel, "so integrity", just doesn't cut it. It leads us right back to happy and Happy. In our minds, we must just make sure to think 'happy' vs. 'Happy' depending on the experience. Then we'll keep things straight. Use other cues if it helps. In my mind, happy is bright, lively, though soon to fade, yellow; Happy is a soothing, everlastingly, pleasing shade of rose.

Of course, happy can come about in a wide variety of ways - and we all need our daily doses of happy. Some 'happies' cost thousands of dollars. Others cost nothing. As far as your mind is concerned, happy is happy. Your happy from a $10,000 ring purchase is perceived by your Deep Mind as equal in every way to your happy from completing a crossword puzzle, enjoying a hand of Hearts, or solving the case in a game of Clue.

How, then, would I utilize all of that information? You're ahead of me, I'm sure. I'd say, since happy is happy why not settle for a few games of Clue and use the ten thousand dollars to feed hungry children or immunize babies in third world countries. That way you get to have happiness plus Happiness, and you've helped make the world a better place along the way.

But you say to me: "I get that happy feeling every time I wear the ring. If I don't have it, I'll miss all those subsequent happies." I'd say to you: "Add scrabble and Canasta to your happiness-providing-repertoire and really enjoy the Happy feeling that comes every time you think about the kids you are helping.

A short detour: A few years ago, I filled in as a 'Big Brother' to an eight-year-old while his usual guy was off on a tour of duty with the Army. He used to introduce me to his buddies with phrases like this. "This is Old Tom. He says a lot of dumb things, but he means well."

His conversation topics centered on hate and revenge and taking what you wanted if you thought you get by with it and staying unhurt and alive on a day to day basis. I talked about love and compassion and being helpful, law abiding, and useful – about building a wonderful future. I imagine those were the dumb things to which he referred, because they were completely foreign to him there in his inner-city neighborhood. The underlying philosophy of living that matched his necessary behavior was quite different from the one that matched mine. He was consumed by just surviving. I was soon consumed by trying to help him survive and grow and develop the desire to make a positive contribution to the world. I learned a lot from him about reality during those six months. I hope he learned a few things about possibilities from me (and my dumb sayings). Fun and happiness to him were seldom experienced, fleeting, moments, during which he felt more or less safe and found a way to possess something (stuff) that brought him pleasure or made him feel important. Improving the world beyond the end of his own nose could never enter his young mind.

If you are reading this book you are different from Carlos in at least one major way; you believe there really is a chance to improve your long-term Happiness. Carlos could only feel helpless. He couldn't buy happiness, let alone Happiness, for any amount.

Detour complete!

Happiness is based in our perception of positive possibilities and our facility for seeing and feeling our fundamental place within the family of man. Being the magnificent human being that you are, came free to you. Happiness, too, is free – it can come in no other way.

For many folks, it requires a substantial reorientation in

the way we think, doesn't it? We tend to believe that more value (cost) equals more Happiness. T'aint so!

Very simply put, each pleasurable event we encounter creates endorphins in our brains. Somewhat simplistically, that process is the basis for our pleasurable feelings. An event that costs nothing produces just as many endorphins as an event that costs a lot. A chuckle, a belly laugh, a present, praise - they are all equal in the brain. The length of time a pleasurable event lasts is the ultimate determiner of how many endorphins are created and therefore how long the happy feelings lasts. Fun creates short term endorphin production and therefore short-term pleasure. Knowing you are living as a relatively good match to your positive philosophy (Integrity) creates a never-ending, steady, 'drip' of endorphins and the resulting controlled sense of euphoria.

Enough about that. I'm sure the points are clear.

1. happy event 1 = happy event 2 = happy event 3, etc.
(With relative cost never entering into the equation.)
2. No amount of happiness, ever = feelings of Happiness.

The title of this chapter suggests we need to take good care of each other. Taking good care includes meeting physical needs (food, clothing, shelter, etc.), state of mind (attitude), safety, companionship, and a host of other things that may be unique to the person or his situation.

"He who does not take care of himself will not be able to take care of others." That piece of great wisdom rode along inside a fortune cookie I once received. Its humble source does not diminish its extraordinary wisdom.

In order to do our good work in this world (thereby achieving our shot at Happiness) we need to take good care of ourselves. We need to maintain our good health, a good mental outlook, a reasonable schedule, time for fun and pleasure, time for me, time to be with friends, spouse, and family. If you're wondering, "When will I have time to do that," begin by cutting out the unnecessary and unrealistic commitments and responsibilities in your life. Make those closest to you your number one priority. Sometimes we train ourselves to believe that if I don't do it nobody else will. In reality, that is almost never true (except position assigned responsibilities within your family). Sometimes we turn our attention to those who are outside our closest circle because we're afraid we might fail our own folks. Sometimes we just don't really think things through at all.

I know a man who had a boat. He was constantly grousing about how much time and effort and expense it took to maintain it. His friends had boats. He used it perhaps a dozen times a year. Not being a boat guy, myself, I asked him what it would cost to rent a similar boat a dozen or so times every summer. Two weeks later he had sold his boat, added many, many hours to use in more constructive ways, and was actually better off financially than he had been before.

I once knew a couple who spent every Thursday evening at 'The Club'. They had dinner, danced, rubbed shoulders with society's upper crust, and engaged in conversations with other members. They hated dressing up. They hated eating where it required six forks. They hated making small talk with people who could never rise above the, who-did-what-to-whom, level of gossipy chit chat. They complained to each other all week about both the past and upcoming Thursday nights. I asked them why they continued to go. "We've paid the membership fee and it's what all our friends do." "Friends?" I asked and let it drop. To my knowledge, they never returned to The Club. Thursday night became family night in their home (something their crowded schedules had never allowed) and after several weeks of screaming protests, their three children (10, 12, and 15) settled into what became a cherished time together for all of them.

I once knew a family - Mom, Pop, Mary, Jim and David. Mom and Pop were up to their armpits in volunteer work for sports, school activities, and so on. (All positive, I'll admit.) Mary and Jim (15 and 11) were becoming behavior problems at school (that's how they came to seek my counsel). After listening to them each describe their family, I made one suggestion and said I'd see them again in two months.

Arrange everybody's busy schedules so they could fix and eat supper together around one table at least six nights a week. Two months later I got a call from the father. "We really don't need to come back, Doc. The problems with the kids just seemed to have disappeared and everything is going great."

I'm not sure if my suggestion was seen as having been helpful (I do know they tried it and seldom missed having supper together from then on) or if they attributed the positive changes to the 'Family Fixing Fairy'. It doesn't matter. By carving out time for each other on a regular basis they healed, both as individuals and as a family.

We need to take good care of each other. That implies another very important side of the coin. We never take advantage of another person. Unfortunately, sometimes that dictum has to be explicitly expanded to: we never take advantage of another person or their hardship.

I do try to keep at least one foot in the realm of reality (despite the dumb things I have been known to say). I do understand that there are thousands upon thousands of people who eagerly, shamelessly, take advantage of others every day.

I was spending the night in a small Kansas town one evening when a tornado hit the south section of the community tearing fifteen homes to shreds and severely damaging several dozen more. The next morning, I had reason to enter the hardware store to purchase a fuse for my dashboard lights. I was appalled at what I saw there. Generators that had been two hundred dollars were marked up to three hundred. Tents and camping supplies had doubled in price. Plastic tarps that originally sold for $3.99 were marked $21.95.

I made my purchase and then asked the proprietor about the price changes.

"Supply and demand," he explained proudly, as if extolling the virtues of some invariant, positive, aspect of the free market economy. For all the great things about a free market economy, when it is not managed with compassion, it can leave a wave of incredible human suffering in its wake. The economy or even one's own pocketbook must never become the bottom line when we approach living from a Positive Personal and Social Philosophy.

"I just don't understand how you can sleep at night gouging your neighbors like this when they are down," I said to the man. "I'd think that you'd want to sell them what they so desperately need at cost or less."

I left, not waiting for a response. I don't know that my remarks changed anything in that man's mind, but I have always appreciated those few minutes with him. He provided me with such a meaningful example of the darkest side of the human psyche - the depths of human greed and the non-compassionate disregard of human suffering.

When one's bottom line becomes a non-negotiable ME and MY welfare or profit regardless of how badly it hurts others, I believe we witness the most despicable side of human nature. I'm bothered by how that very line of thinking seems to be rampant in big business and financial circles around the globe today. "Benefit me at any and all costs to others."

(I just shuddered at the thought. I hope you did, too!)

Take good care of yourself so you can take good care of your closest loved ones. Then, spend some time and effort, and perhaps even some money, helping those who are a step or so removed from your inner circle. How can that not help but benefit you, your family, humankind, and the world? The 'match' that comes from that approach to living will - guaranteed - plant a smile on your face and keep it glowing in your heart forever.

When people ask me, "What's got you all smiles today?" I answer, "Match induced endorphins, thank you," and go on my way feeling sinfully smug about just having lived up to the essence of a Carlos introduction.

EXERCISE:

Revisit the previous exercises and see if you can improve on or need to revise any of those responses.

///

CHAPTER NINE
SECRET 7
Replace Worrying with Planning

I was eight and was proudly riding my 'new' bike (a unique looking vehicle, which I had just built out of parts scrounged from here and there). That early morning maiden voyage took me down the dirt road toward Miller's farm. The night before, we had experienced what we kids called, a Dry Lightning Blower – unending lightning and ferocious wind but not a drop of rain. It was a regular July phenomenon in the upper Midwest. So was the resulting scramble of young boys seeking safe haven beneath their beds as such events rolled in.

It had been no more than a half hour later when dawn broke and I mounted my new ride. The road was strewn with small branches, leaves, and freshly mown hay that would miss its scheduled rendezvous with the bailer later that day.

I came upon a small section of barbed wire fence that had been blown over and twisted. Mr. Miller was walking down the road toward me as I approached and stopped. There were two animals standing there with their front legs entangled in the wire – a horse named Ribbon and donkey named Donkey.

"Good morning, Mr. Miller."

"Good morning, Master Tommy," (It was how he talked.)

"Looks like a big problem, Sir."

"Only for Ribbon."

"How so?" I asked, puzzled.

"Horses get hung up like that and they worry themselves into all kinds of pain and badly torn flesh – pulling and tugging with no plan. See how the Jack Ass is just standing there quietly. It'll soon figure out it just needs to lift its leg straight up and it'll be unharmed and free."

I waited and watched. Mr. Miller had been right. We had to help Ribbon, or he'd have torn his leg to shreds. As predicted the Jack Ass worked it out by himself.

So, my hope for you is that you will go through life as a Jack Ass. (Perhaps, some explanation is in order!)

When we worry, we rehash some unpleasantry or the possibility of some future unpleasantry with no intention of creating a solution. We just rehash for the sake of rehashing.

Sometimes we trick ourselves into believing we are looking for a plan by saying, "I just don't know what I'm going to do." Embracing the not knowing defense is seldom a constructive way to begin solving a problem.

If we were to again draw a long line and divide it into four equal sections and label one end Worrying and the other Planning, we could locate where our typical approach to problems sits between the two extremes.

Worry restates the problem and reinforces our unhappy - sometimes overwhelming - feelings. Those cause the most intense kind of tension which, as we know, reduces our efficiency and our ability to think clearly. Worrying always sends us into a useless, downward, emotional, spiral.

Planning, on the other hand, moves us from the helpless realm into the realm of possibilities. Some of our plans may not work. Some will be abandoned before we even try them, but plans represent the possibility of solutions rather than inevitable, unending, despair of worry. They suggest that we are working to take control of our destiny rather than just sitting back to let come what will. Planning eases tension because our Deep Mind senses that we are working with it to survive and not just giving into defeat (death, in terms of the Deep Mind's simple way of configuring things).

There are several ways of defeating worry. The best is to begin by finding the source or sources of the worry.

Sometimes that isn't possible.

Old Mrs. Stephens was my neighbor when I was a little boy. She rocked her life away on her front porch worrying about the fact that sometime in the near future she would die.

Naively, I once gave her my take on her situation. "If you're going to die soon, I'd think you'd want to work hard at really enjoying every day you have left."

"You just don't understand."

Apparently not. When sad times came my way I used Mom's plan - overpower it, push it aside, and bury it under heaps of happiness. The method was simple. When I began feeling down about something, I'd get out games, I'd ride my bike, I'd begin building a new something-or-other, or I'd go help out one of our neighbors. When Mom or Pop sensed my plummeting mood, they'd set me to work on something that engaged my brain - distracting it away from POOR ME to something more pressing and inviting or useful.

When I verbalized worry, Dad would say, "So, what are you doing to fix it?"

I learned that some things can't be fixed so some other tack needed to be taken. I was always the littlest guy in my class at school. I hung from the monkey bars hours on end hoping that would stretch me. I avoided jumping off high places thinking the impact might compact me even further. I tried shaving (years ahead of any actual need) thinking I might fool my body into thinking it needed to grow fast in order to catch up with my hormones. None of that worked. (Imagine that!!!)

I confronted Dad about it. He had a pair of questions for me.

"Do you worry because broccoli isn't ice cream?"

"Of course, not!"

"Why don't you?"

"Because you can't just make changes like that happen. . . Oh! . . . Thanks, Dad."

I never worried about my height again. I was what I was and that was that. (By eighth grade I settled in at six feet.) I was suddenly free to attack the really important issues in my life (How to convince Mary Beth to kiss me! How to help

Butchie stop stealing things. How to bring some joy into Old Mrs. Stephens' life. What wonderful gift to make Mom for her birthday.)

All of this rambling really has a point. It suggests the several kinds or levels of things about which we find ourselves worrying. Some can be more or less easily solved. Some can be solved eventually - perhaps after seeking additional information. Some need time or natural development to occur, before they can be solved. A few can probably not be solved. (These often include things that happened in the past or conditions existing far away.)

It provides such a feeling of power when we move a situation from the Worry category into the Planning category. We instantaneously go from helpless to powerful! Helpless is always a sad situation. Powerful, is typically a happy if not a Happy situation. If our plan succeeds, our spirits soar. If our plan fails, we have the opportunity to try something new, now knowing what would not work – something we could not have known had we not made the attempt. At worst, we can say, "I tired," and that is always a plus in terms of self-worth.

There are times we find ourselves worrying about somebody else: Will they make the right decision about something? Or, they made a bad choice and now have to accept the unpleasant consequences.

Those things need to be elevated out of the abyss of worry up to the level of concern. We can feel compassion and move on without allowing ourselves to wallow in the other person's problem - worry about it. We can't live another's life for him (and shouldn't if I'm allowed a value statement). Sometimes, however, there are things we can do. We have to learn the difference.

Once in a while Old Mrs. Stephens would call Mom and ask if I could come over to her house for a little while. "I always feel so good after he's been here," she'd admit to Mom.

The old lady and I both felt the power. She was taking control of her 'blues' by asking me over. I was helping my dear old friend feel better. Truly, at six, I had no idea what I was doing to make the improvement. I asked Mom what I should do while I was there.

"Don't be concerned about being any special way. Just be yourself. That's all it seems to take."

I'll tell you for sure, I put such energy into just being myself that the earth shook beneath our feet!!!

Make a list of your worries. Be specific. "Not enough money to pay the bills." "Jim seems to be pulling away from me." "Billy has begun acting up in the classroom." "I'm worried about Mary's current choice of boyfriend." "My parents will soon be unable to care for themselves."

Then, pick out three that have elements in them that you may be able to control. Select one of them and begin brainstorming. Let's use the money/bills as an example.

The options seem obvious. Either reduce bills or increase money.

I can reduce bills by driving less - better organizing my necessary coming and going. Maybe work out a car-pooling arrangement with other mothers to get my kids to and from school, and activities. We can fix meals at home more often. The kids can begin earning some of their allowance by helping with the lawn work, so we don't have to pay to have it done. We can live with fewer new clothes and certainly fewer designer fashions. Perhaps I can refinance my car or home for smaller monthly payments, or search out lower rate credit cards and transfer some of my debt to them, etc.

I can increase my income by taking that early morning paper route, cleaning houses on Saturday mornings, baking specialty cakes and cookies for parties, marrying George Clooney/Julia Roberts, etc.

For many middle-class folks, worry often stems from chasing that which is unnecessary, frivolous, and extravagant (clearly, my evaluation). Look to your positive personal and social philosophy and begin to pare away at your expectations until you have done away with the excesses. (More in Chapter fourteen.)

When worries revolve around things that are not required for your Deep Down Forever Happiness, make arrangements for getting rid of them. Most certainly if they revolve around things you acquired to 'make yourself Happy' get rid of them (Well, you can keep your spouse or significant other, I suppose!).

We'll speak at length later about downsizing possessions in the service of happiness. The general rule is: Stuff equals added responsibility, added power usage, ongoing expenses, excess refuse, more space, and maintenance related work. You have to determine whether the added burdens are really worth it. Remember that you most certainly don't need to have stuff just to impress others if you are accepting the foundations of this program. You don't need their approval - especially when they are offering their approval of you on the basis of the quality or amount of the stuff you possess.

Typically, it comes down to less stuff, less worry, and more time and money. Less worry translates into more happiness and more time to work on the BIG H - Deep Down Forever Happiness.

I've known many people whose main worry was that they were not Happy. In my experience, it is the easiest worry to solve. Replace their present goals with Integrity and their present negative or vague philosophy with a specifically stated Positive Philosophy, and that worry WILL evaporate almost immediately.

EXERCISE:

If you are a worrier, take time to make a detailed list of the specific things about which you are worrying. As suggested above, begin attacking them one at a time trying to make the worry evaporate by replacing it with a plan.

When your analysis reveals there is nothing you can do about some worry topic, move it to your OOMC (double Oh MC) list. It stands for Out Of My Control. You probably can't stop the warring factions in Africa. You probably can't stop North Korea or Iran from doing whatever evil things they seem bent on doing. You can't remove all the scoundrels from congress or even local government. Dwell on those things and you will feel both helpless and depressed and become immobilized so you can't work on the easier (possible) things.

Set the OOMCs aside and get to work on things over

which you can realistically gain some control. I can only guess at your worries. The family budget, increasing time together as a family, making life easier or more pleasant for the old couple next door, the safety and well-being of your children or older parents, beefing up security in your home or neighborhood, welcoming your kids' friends into your home (so you know where they are and what they are doing), gradually introducing more healthful food into your loved ones diets, downsizing your life into a comfortable, more worry free, easier to handle, existence, and so on.

Devise a plan. Work the plan. Modify or replace the plan if necessary. Solve the problem. Evaporate the worry. In other words, become a World Class Jack Ass!

///

CHAPTER TEN
SECRET 8
Replace 'Blame and Punish' with 'Find Out and Fix'

There are two basic approaches we can use when we find ourselves in positions where we must handle a problem involving a person who has erred in some fashion. (When we are in the role of disciplinarian, parent, or other peacekeeper, for example.) A third approach is also possible - The Ignoring it All approach but that is seldom fruitful, and we won't linger over it here.

Approach One: Most of us have grown up in a blame and punish environment - if not within our family, then in society as a whole. Jimmy broke the lamp, so he gets grounded. Billy started the fight, so he gets a spanking. Mary called Beth a bad name, so she gets extra chores. Tom sold drugs so he gets sent to jail. Mom left her small children alone in a car on a hot summer day, so she gets sent to jail. Bobby picked up a 'no-no' from the coffee table so he got his 13-month-old hands slapped. Blame and punishment permeate our society and contribute heavily to the aggressive, hurtful, way of life we witness today - the one in which human life becomes valueless and one takes whatever he is powerful or sly enough to take.

Approach Two: Some of us have been fortunate enough to have grown up - at least within our home - in a Find Out and Fix environment. Jimmy broke the lamp, so Mom investigates how it came about and takes steps to help Jimmy avoid doing similar things in the future. Billy started a fight so Dad investigates how it came about and takes steps to help Billy find other ways of solving disagreements with his age mates. Mary called Beth a bad name, so Mom investigates and helps Mary find more appropriate alternatives. Tom sold drugs so his social worker investigates and determines that if he had a job he would not have sold. She finds him a job. Mom left her small children alone in a car on hot summer day. The investigator found an emotionally fragile mother distraught over a divorce, poverty, four needy, demanding children, and loss of her job, and worked with her to set her life back on track so things such as her children's welfare could come first again. Bobby lived in a home that understood his still developing young brain was way too immature at 13 months of age to fully understand about no-nos so the lower three feet of the house was pretty well free of them.

I think it's a law of human nature: The easiest way to do something is typically found to be ineffective or second rate in the end. To merely find out who is to blame and then punish him is the easy - lazy - way to go about enforcing a set of values - rules or laws in the larger sense. It becomes the rule that is more important than the child. It takes no parenting know-how to beat a kid or ground him when he breaks a rule (a rule he may not have even known existed until he broke it). It takes no study of child development to just blame and punish. It's easier to blame and punish than it is to learn and apply the principles of encouraging and teaching positive interpersonal relationships. The bottom line here is that punishing kids and others has never been known to improve one's Deep Down Forever Happiness (for either the punished or the punisher).

As a young, wet behind the ears, psychologist, I once passionately proposed to a state legislature that before citizens were allowed to get married they should be required to pass a test covering what was known for sure about maintaining positive interpersonal relations and raising well adjusted, mentally healthy, children. I referenced it to that State's requirement for passing tests to use a gun, drive a car, skiing, and to be certified to practice in a number of professional capacities (doctor, lawyer, etc.). It seemed to me that marriage and child rearing were certainly more important than those things. I was laughed off the podium.

Since half the children born in our country today are born to unmarried mothers, such a system would not have helped for long even if it had been enacted. The saddest element in it all is, I believe, that most people don't even know that such tried and proven information is available. The evidence is irrefutable. Go about raising children in one way and they are in for a lifetime of hurt and disappointment. Raise them another way and they are almost certain to become a loving, mentally healthy, law abiding, productive, part of society and eventually of their own families. [See books such as: Trouble-Proofing Kids by this author and One Rule Plan for Family Happiness]

Where is this leading? The blame and punish approach has seldom ever been known to really solve a problem and folks who have seriously studied interpersonal relationships, parenting, and social planning know that. Do you suppose schools need to be teaching that instead of second year algebra to young people who will never use that skill? Let's take an educated look at punishment.

True, as human beings, we avoid pain and discomfort when we can. (Our Deep Mind requires that, remember?) The threat of Pain and discomfort should, one might think, whip folks into line in a hurry. That's what we are led to believe. It often does . . . when the one with authority to punish is close enough to monitor the behavior. Nowhere is the old adage, Out of sight, out of mind, more applicable than with rule enforcement by punishment. Kids don't take cookies out of the cookie jar when Mom's there. Are they more likely to when she isn't? Drivers don't speed when there is a policeman in view. Are they more likely to when he isn't? Clerks don't put company stamps on their personal envelopes when the boss is around. Are they more likely to when he isn't?

When we expect members of our society to abide by rules and laws out of fear of punishment you can bet it won't work to make a happy, comfortable, trusting, mutually helpful, social order. Even in police states where citizens' every activity is monitored, it doesn't work. Line criminals up in front of public firing squads and there continues to be crime. Punishment is not the answer to an improved social order (or family life).

I've known families in which Dad or Mom ruled with an iron fist and the kids were model citizens. When they got out on their own (work or college) they went wild, breaking rules, disrespecting others, and often ruining their own chances for a bright future by getting into serious trouble. Others were incapacitated with intense fears and phobias. Why? Largely because they had never been helped to learn how to set appropriate rules for themselves, to look ahead to the possible consequences, or monitor their own behavior. They developed no positive values toward which to strive - to guide them - to live by. They only learned what was not acceptable to somebody else. Do you see any Deep Down Forever Happiness blossoming from such an arrangement?

Contrast them with kids from homes in which positive values were modeled and kids were helped to develop a positive (what I should do) philosophy. In both cases, the kid's made mistakes along the way. In case one, the kids were punished. In case two, the kids were helped to analyze how the problem had developed and determine what to do differently next time so it wouldn't have to happen again. The children grew in knowledge and wisdom, and their positive philosophy gained breadth and width. (Can you see the seeds of Deep Down Forever Happiness there?)

So long as one clings to the Blame and Punish philosophy (and the hurtful behavior that necessarily follows) he is going to be disappointed with his own long-term success in controlling (teaching?) others and with the ultimate quality of self-control and personal development in those he has tried to influence.

Is it easier to just blame and punish? You bet it is! Is it the absolutely least effective, most harmful, way to interact with others? You bet it is! (The easiest route is typically not the best route, remember.)

So, Secret Number Eight for Deep Down Forever

Happiness tells us to diminish our 'Who Should be Blamed and Punished' impulses and behaviors. It tells us to replace that approach with the expert administration of the 'What Needs to Be Fixed?' approach. By the way, this applies both to the ways we approach others as well as ourselves.

Some people have great difficulty making that change in orientation. That is most likely because we have been steeped for so long in the idea that for some mystical and unjustified reason misbehavior just always requires punishment. In the back of our heads we may also hope that it teaches the offender a positive lesson (which it doesn't) but basically, we have come to believe that misbehavior deserves punishment for no greater reason other than that it was misbehavior. Punish first (always), then, maybe if there is social motivation or sufficient government funding, make some attempt at rehabilitation.

During my stint in the early grades, I spent a LOT of time in the principal's office. It wasn't because I hurt or bullied anybody. It wasn't that I broke the rules any more often than my classmates. It was because I had a hard time holding my young tongue when the teachers did or said really dumb things, or when they disrespected one of their students. I'd stand on my seat and rant and rave at the teacher for the injustice I believed I was witnessing.

My principal was a dear, wise, old, soul. In most lower grade rooms, there are two, finger signals. One finger if you have to go to the rest room and stay only a minute or so. Two if you have to go and stay a while longer. Principal Evans initiated a three-finger signal system in my room – number three, just for me. It signaled the teacher that Tommy was about to blow his young top about something and was requesting to go to the principal's office before it happened.

It worked like a charm. I got to go vent to Mr. Evans who, unlike the teachers, listened to me. It allowed him to offer gentle counsel and provide reading material on topics related to my seething young sense of injustice. Without him ever disagreeing with or putting down any of the teachers, I always felt like he was on my side. Unlike most boys, I suppose, many of my fondest memories from grade school come from the time I spent in the Office. (I also learned that, contrary to the big boy's fear-filled stories, there was no electric paddling machine in there!)

The Find Out and Fix approach is basically true to a Positive Philosophy/Integrity/Behavior Matching Plan for living. We locate what went wrong (perhaps, what happened that is not a match to a positive philosophy or rule) and then find ways of making it more likely that on future occasions the behavior will be in accord with that positive philosophy or value.

In the Blame and Punish approach, we first put the misbehaver down (blame) and then we set out to hurt him or make him feel bad or less adequate (punishment). There is just nothing in that approach that meshes with the kind of Positive Philosophy, which we are investigating here. If I put somebody down does that make a match to any element in a positive philosophy? If I hurt somebody physically or emotionally does that make a match to any element in a positive philosophy?

What does growing up under each of the two approaches teach us about the world and its people?

The Blame and Punish approach demonstrates that people are hurtful and that is a frightening realization with which to have to cope throughout one's life. It provides no guidance about what to do to live a happy and productive life. It leaves the deep-down impression that the world is not a friendly, hopeful, helpful, dependable, safe place.

The Find and Fix approach demonstrates that people are helpful and want the best for you, that they are willing to go out of their way to teach and assist in your positive growth. It instills hope. Clearly, they want to help you learn how to have a comfortable and successful life. It leaves the deep-down impression that at least your part of the world is a friendly, dependable, helpful, place.

To apply the Find Out and Fix Approach with children, it is often as simple as helping them answer a question like: "What rule do you need to make for yourself so you will be able to handle things like that better (more acceptably) next time?"

To apply this approach to yourself ask the same question and then move on to searching for an inappropriate Deep Mind Directive that may be keeping you from being able to demonstrate the more positive behavior you desire. (Finally, the next chapter offers specific instructions!!! You have been soooooooo patient.)

EXERCISE:

It's time for another set of lists. This time use two sheets of paper. Label one, Blame and Punish Approach (BAP). The other, Find Out and Fix Approach (FOF). On the FOF sheet just list the instances when you approached a problem in that positive way. Give yourself a huge mental gold star for each.

Split the BAP sheet in half, right and left, from top to bottom. In the left column enter the instances when you approached a problem in the BAP way. In the right column rewrite the instance suggesting a way you could have approached it using the FOF approach. Note any additional information you may need to acquire to knowledgeably help fix things.

During each day think BAP! or FOF! as you approach your dealings with others.

CHAPTER ELEVEN
SECRET 9
Rearranging Your Deep Mind
(For the better!!)

First, let's review the previous eight secrets. Each of them provides important information, the mastery of which is necessary before the techniques presented in this chapter can become useful.

Secret One: Never expect your Deep Down Forever Happiness to flow from stuff, money, power, or winning. Deep Down Happiness is absolutely free and non-competitive in nature.

Secret Two: Develop, understand, and practice a positive social philosophy (giving not taking, helping not hurting).

Secret Three: Live a life of Integrity (always living up to your own positive value system - philosophy).

Secret Four: You only ever really need to have your own approval to be Deep Down Happy.

Secret Five: Reduce Selfism. Increase Altruism.

Secret Six: Routinely take good care of yourself and those with whom you come in contact. Begin by reducing gruffness and isolation and increasing kindness and interest.

Secret Seven: Replace worrying with planning.

Secret Eight: Replace the always destructive, go nowhere, Blame and Punish (BAP) approach with the usually helpful, What needs to be fixed? (FOF) technique.

The four secrets that follow this chapter are also essential for the full utilization of the techniques included here but I have decided to present the techniques and then in the subsequent chapters provide exercises to help you master their use.

Let us begin this presentation by reviewing and explaining some essential characteristics of the Deep Mind. Briefly, think of your mind as having three levels: There is the Surface or conscious mind of which you are most aware. It allows you to think, perceive what's around you, remember, talk, walk, and so on. The Deep Mind, of which you are typically not aware, is the center that drives you as a person through the Directives stored there. In all struggles between so called 'Will Power' (Surface Mind) and Deep Mind Directives, the Deep Mind, always, eventually, wins. (More a bit later.) There is a third function of the Mind, which I refer to as the Great Filter. Think of it as sitting like a fine mesh screen between the Surface Mind and the Deep Mind. It scans and analyses the perceptions and thoughts of the Surface Mind (conscious mind) and decides what it is going to allow to enter (filter down to) the Deep Mind. One of its functions is to keep from upsetting the Deep Mind with information that is contrary to what is already stored there. The Great Filter's motto is, "Don't rock the Deep Mind's boat." That both helps and hinders. It is why we need to learn specific techniques for approaching (getting through to) the Deep Mind.

The Surface Mind is capable of using logic and language – its two crowning achievements, most believe. The Deep Mind functions not by logic but by correlation. It was mentioned earlier. When two things occur together the Deep Mind believes they have a bond of some kind. When something occurs right after a first event, the Deep Mind typically believes the first caused the second. (Flip a switch and a light comes on. Dad drinks, then he beats me. When I enter the house after school Mom hugs me and I feel loved and safe. There is a cause and effect bond or expectation established.)

The Surface Mind relies most heavily on words - its verbal skills. It is most comfortable in that realm. The Deep Mind does poorly with words. It prefers images and emotions.

The Deep Mind only considers positive information. (Do such and such - never, don't do such and such.) It typically turns negatives into positives and then proceeds accordingly. ("Don't talk to the new kids who moved in next door." Yeah! Right!!)

Each experience of which the Deep Mind becomes aware and each suggestion it hears get stored as what I call Directives (because they urge us to take some action). A Directive is a tendency to behave, again, in a certain manner. Picture the Deep Mind as a massive set of cubby holes like found in a post office sorting room. Each slot contains a card with just one entry on it. You will learn how to change the positions of those cards (directives) from more likely to occur to less likely. You will learn how to get rid of directive that you don't want managing your life, and you will learn how to create and plant new directives that you do want to have helping you run your life.

As long as we are pretending (giving a physical structure to your Deep Mind that is for illustrative purposes only) paint the top row of cubby holes bright red. Those will be the places you store the most important aspects of your Positive Personal Philosophy of Living - behaviors (directives) that you want to have propelling you through your day to day encounters with other people and yourself.

The cards are continually shifting from hole to hole depending on several things. Those toward the beginning of the set of cubbies are most likely to be used by the Deep Mind. There are several ways of assuring certain directives remain easily at hand.

Those directives that have been reviewed, used, or received most recently tend to remain in the ready-to-use section. Also, those that are set in place accompanied by great emotion tend to remain in those early compartments (often becoming nearly impossible to move out). So, recently set directives and those set with great emotion tend to be the directives of choice by the Deep Mind.

The Deep Mind loves short, concise, communiqués - preferably questions and never direct commands. The Deep Mind believes it is the center of the universe and who in their right mind would think the Center of the Universe would succumb to someone else's dictums? (Example: rather than saying to your Deep Mind, "Make me act with patience toward Bobby today" (a command), try something like, "How can I act with patience toward Bobby today?" (a question) It changes the command to a question and immediately moves the comment from Deep Mind rejection to eager, action-oriented, acceptance.

The Deep Mind loves to work on questions and solve problems. Since it never sleeps, like the rest of your mind has to, it's available 24/7 to help you. Ask it a short, well phrased, question just before you go to sleep at night, and it will work its little heart out searching for an answer while the rest of you gets your beauty rest. (We have all experienced times when we couldn't remember someone's name and a few minutes or hours later it popped into our consciousness? Guess 'who' was continuing its work for you even after the 'rest of you' moved on to other matters!)

There is one more important piece of background information you need to know before we get down to work on the techniques. When your body relaxes so does that Great Filter I described. Since it has to relax in order for you to contact your Deep Mind directly, you must master the muscle relaxation technique presented earlier in the book. There is no reason to try the technique without having first done that!

Picture it this way. Tension pulls the filter's 'wire mesh' tight, making the openings small and ridged. Relaxing lets that mesh sag and droop and increases the size of the openings so more kinds of things can penetrate it.

Here, then, are the basic steps necessary for speaking directly with your Deep Mind.

1. Relax deeply.

2. Use simple, precise, phrases.

3. Use questions when you can. (Rather than saying, "Help me get to sleep, now!" try something like, "What needs to be taking place within me so I can fall into a restful sleep?

Can you help me do that, please?")

4. A single presentation of a clear question is enough. (Each stating of a question is seen as a brand-new item. There is no reason to have your Deep Mind working on four questions that are all really the same question. In fact, such replication is confusing because it tries to search out differences among them - differences, which in that case, do not or should not exist.)

5. Whenever possible, approach the Deep Mind with Images and Feelings instead of - or along with - words. The Deep Mind is an image-based function rather than a verbal-based function (unlike the Surface Mind). In your mind's eye, see yourself acting in ways you want to be directed to act (images). Feel how you want to feel when behaving in certain ways (emotions).

6. Approach your Deep Mind politely. It has to first determine if any incoming message holds some threat to its person. Polite is generally considered pretty much threat free. (The Con Artist certainly understands this, doesn't he?) The Deep Mind cannot act effectively and efficiently for you if it is tied up with the tension it experiences when taking the necessary steps to defend you from possible threats.

Now, to the technique. In my book, The Secrets of Deep Mind Mastery, you will find many other ways to assist your Deep Mind. The 'Movie Screen' technique presented here is quite versatile and should serve you well in managing your typical Directives.

Earlier, you made a list of traits (behaviors, directives) you wish were not a part of your personality - the way you approach life. You need to select one of those. Think about it and describe what you want in its place. You will be getting rid of the unwanted directive and adding or strengthening the one you do want.

Next, let me describe the setting you will need to establish in the imagination of your mind's eye. It is the inside of a small movie theater. The front of the room is a wall to wall screen. It is glowing a pleasant light blue and provides a soothing, low level of light throughout the room. At a comfortable distance from the screen, in the center of the seating section is a blue recliner. It will be extremely comfortable. Ease into the immediately inviting, cozy, chair. Near the front of the arm of the chair (the arm for your dominant hand) there is a joystick that moves front to back. In a comfortable spot on top of that stick, at a place easily covered by your thumb, is a red button. While holding the stick, your thumb will easily be able to press it. The room becomes darker. Safe and dark. Relaxed and dark. You can only really see the screen, which is glowing softly, filling the wall in front on you.

You will now create two collages (a number of pictures collected on one sheet) in your mind. One will include pictures illustrating the unwanted trait. Some may pop to mind immediately from past experiences. Some you may just make up. Each one should illustrate something about the unwanted trait – most helpfully, a picture of you engaging in it. Remember these have to be your traits. You can't use this technique to change any force outside of yourself or within anybody else. Paint those pictures with bright colors and fill them with the intense, unpleasant, pulsing, emotions that emerge as you think back on them. Work at it until you have several representative pictures constructed on that page – a totally disturbing collage. Then lay it aside.

Relax. Take a couple of comfortably deep breaths. Clear your mind. Now, repeat the process, but this time make the collage representative of the positive trait you want to set into your Deep Mind to replace the one you were just working on. Again, use bright colors. Put yourself in the display acting the way you want to act. Fill it all with wonderfully positive, happy, contented, comfortable, successful feelings. Make them powerfully positive! The inner feeling should be wonderful. It should be impossible to keep a smile from breaking across your face. Then, put that picture aside.

The success of this technique depends on the absolute appropriateness of each collage. Spend time carefully planning each one. Take hours if necessary. Be Precise. Be vivid. Be complete. Use the most meaningful and representative images you can discover or create. They can be still images or can be mini movies in which you see yourself in action. (Study the three preceding paragraphs until you have mastered every last syllable.)

It will take just one minute now to give you the nuts and bolts necessary to put all this to work for you. First, you will be asked to put the negative collage up on the screen across the front wall. (Not now.) You will be asked to feel the emotions and the intensity of everything uncomfortable about it. Then you will be instructed to move the joystick forward. That reduces the size of the picture from full wall down to the size of a postage stamp up there in the middle of the screen. Next you will press the red button with your thumb. That will blow the stamp-sized image into a billion pieces and activate a swirling wind that will pick up the pieces and carry them all through the roof distributing them to the four corners of the globe. Gone forever! Immediately, you will then slowly pull the joystick back toward you. Your second collage (positive) will come up on the screen along with the dramatic change in feelings from unpleasantly negative to wonderfully positive. Leave it there full sized in front of you for some time searching it with your eyes and enjoying the feelings. See yourself as you want to be. Experience the feelings you want to feel. When you want the collage to fade away and have the screen resume its pleasing light blue glow, just remove your hand from the joystick.

Once you have carefully and expertly constructed your two very best image collages and filled them with the most appropriate and intense emotions, you are ready to begin. After you have finished a sequence, wait at least a half hour before working on replacing and adding another set of traits.

Remember the steps.

1- Relax comfortably and deeply. Take whatever time you need to establish this essential state of mind and body. Sitting in an armchair that mimics the one you are envisioning may help.

2- See the negative images across the huge screen and feel the negative emotions rushing out at you. Study it for at least a minute. It should be a very uncomfortable minute! This is your good-bye visit with that trait (Directive).

3- Push the joystick forward and shrink the image so

small you can hardly see it as a speck on the screen. It is as if those images have been pulled - sucked – right out of your mind and onto the screen.

4- Push the button and explode the negative image and watch it disappear forever in the whirlwind.

5- Then, pull the stick back toward you and watch the wonderful, positive, collage come into full view. Feel the accompanying powerful positive emotions as they over-power the others. Sit there enjoying it for as long as you like.

If you want to repeat the process for that same pair of negative / positive traits you may do so (although it probably won't be necessary if you achieved full relaxation and if you constructed a truly powerful presentation). If you do it again, be sure that you make this one change in the subsequent exposures. Each time you begin the sequence, make sure that first negative screen starts out as a smaller image than it was the time before. Much of that directive (probably almost all of it) will be gone so never bring it back full sized. Even half size will probably be way too much. A larger image will really confuse the Deep Mind. On the other hand, the Positive images should continue to be made as huge and colorful, and powerful as your theater screen will allow. (It is best to do a great job the first time and let it go.)

Repeat the technique with other directives that need your attention – always at least twenty-four hours apart.

Technique two: Your daily tune-up

Select three or four - no more than six - positive traits (directives) from your Positive Personal Philosophy. Make them the ones you feel are most important in guiding your everyday interactions with others. Distill them each down to a few simple words. When they are simple enough, they don't have to be in question form. For example, you might prepare a statement: "I feel safe, fulfilled, and happy when I act with compassion and helpfulness." In that case compassion and helpfulness are the directives you are reminding your Deep Mind about. You are imbuing them with feelings, which are also high on the Deep Minds list of good stuff - safe, fulfilled, and happy.

Now, how do you use all this? As you prepare to drift off to sleep (probably at night) pull up some really great feelings. Then, repeat your phrase slowly and meaningfully. You can repeat it several times as you feel yourself relaxing more and more. Then let a comfortable blue cloud encompass you and go to sleep.

Why do this Daily Tune Up? Remember, the Deep Mind tends to act on the most recent directives it believes it has received from you. Doing it daily keeps those directives in its 'ready for action' cubbies, available to be pulled up and used as situations arise.

Try this variation with your children as they make ready to leave for school or go out to play. The secret here is to make them provide the directives - not you. Rather than reminding them to behave themselves (immediately rejected as a command by their Deep Mind) ask: "What kind of a guy are you going to try to be today, Tommy?"

Get a real answer (not settling for the first, Smart Alecky, comeback you may receive). Follow it with a hug or kiss or whatever method you regularly use to remind your child how precious he is and how much you love him.

You have just successfully utilized the two most powerful techniques for reinforcing a Deep Mind Directive – recency and emotion.

In our home, we usually took it a step further. During breakfast (which we arranged to eat together at the kitchen table) we would each name someone in our outside-of-our-home life that we were going to try and help that day. Sometimes we added how we hoped to accomplish it. Sometimes we kept that to ourselves. Bottom line: it energized our Deep Mind's positive juices early every single day. Sometimes we'd seek to enlist each other's help with our 'project person'.

So, rid your Deep Mind of Directives you don't want to have running your life. Replace them with positive Directives you do want to have guiding your way of living. Review frequently with your Deep Mind, the several directives that seem most important - most basic. (Rotate them from day to day if the list includes more than four or five.)   Enjoy the resulting Happiness!

EXERCISE:

Practice, practice, practice!   (Never share the Movie Screen Technique with anyone who has not read this book! Phrased in a way the Deep Mind will accept it, that precaution becomes: "Always make sure that anybody who tries the Movie Screen Technique has read this book first!)   Managing ones Deep Mind is Serious Business.

CHAPTER TWELVE
SECRET TEN
Seeing Failures as Successes

Actually, this chapter will discuss two issues, the one stated above and another important concept we can refer to as, "Different doesn't necessarily equal Bad".

They each present a major hurdle for many folks. The first - Failure - presents an ongoing contest against all those stored Directives that relate to being successful, doing well, being perfect, or keeping others happy by our mastery of all that we encounter. The second - Different - runs absolutely contrary to our Deep Mind's Prime Directive - "Keep my person safe" - so that one takes some doing even under the best of circumstances.

Let's examine the second one, first. In order to fulfill that prime purpose, the Deep Mind must treat every new experience, person, and idea, with suspicion until it is satisfied that it is safe for you to approach or engage it. That is similar, I assume, to the way you evaluate your children's new acquaintances, dates, and so on, as you strive to keep your children safe and protected. The Great Filter does its best to sort out that which is just too different so as to not confuse or challenge the Deep Mind.

When the Deep Mind sees something 'Different' it builds a wall to keep whatever it is at a distance. The more it learns about the new thing, the better it can form a realistic picture of its safety factor. Eventually, it may welcome it with open neurons but until then it will be cautiously conservative in its evaluation.

Some of us have been taught to reject people and ideas and methods that are different from how 'we' are or how 'we' do things. In such situations, there is little if any effort made to find things out about the new entity. "Reject it and keep your distance," becomes the entire, forever, motto.

On the other hand, many of us have been taught to eagerly take steps to learn more about that which is different, to see what wonderful things we may able to learn from it, and to ferret out just what things we have in common with it.

So, some of us automatically reject 'different' because of its possible harm factor (mimicking how the Deep Mind operates). Others of us have learned to embrace and examine 'different' for its potential benefits. (Engaging a grand capacity of our uniquely human conscious mind – the Surface Mind).

With minimal logical capacities, the Deep Mind cannot easily analyze 'Different'. It uses correlation and assumes that since 'Different' is often paired with harm or disaster, anything different must be kept at arm's length. Fortunately, we humans have that surface - conscious - mind that can move well beyond correlation. It can gather data and ascertain the probable degree of danger or safety contained within most 'Differents' that we encounter.

Unfortunately, the Deep Mind's prime directive paves the way for uneducated prejudice - uneducated meaning lack of the unbiased exploration of whatever 'Different' is at hand. It says, "He's different so stay away from him." For what may be a fascinating, 'Aha!' experience for you, replace the word, different, with things that are the stuff of prejudice - black, white, liberal, conservative, right wing, left wing, lawyer, shrink, Middle Easterner, Westerner, Writers of Happiness books, and so on. It is the conscious mind that adds those labels. As far as the Deep Mind is concerned, initially, they all mean the same thing - Different - and therefore potentially dangerous.

A mind filled with intense biases against one or more categories of 'Differents' is a tension filled mind. When we reject a 'Different' it is because we are convinced it probably poses a threat to us - usually because we just don't know enough about it. When somebody says, "I reject all green skinned men because they are no good," he is really saying, "I reject all green skinned men because my Deep Mind fears potential harm from them and I'm going along with it." (Probably without any honest, personal investigation.)

Fear is readily merged with hate in the emotional stew of the Deep Mind. Hate is one of the action emotions we use to overcome or destroy sources of fear (a labeling emotion).

So, what's the point? A person obsessed with the fear or hate of 'Different' (seeing 'Different' as Bad) exists in a sea of irresolvable, negative, tension. Hate and fear are not positive forces. A life guided by hate or fear or the idea that 'Different' is bad, cannot be guided by a positive philosophy. He or she can therefore never find Deep Down Forever Happiness, the way this book characterizes it. People with such deep 'anti-something' biases (prejudices) have to spend more and more time stockpiling evidence (fact or fiction) to support their point of view, so, quite predictably, they most often sink into an inefficient and ineffective way of living.

Sometimes, 'Different" may actually be dangerous (bad) and does need to be avoided (terrorists, pedophiles, drug pushers, and so on). My caution is that you thoroughly evaluate each instance on its own merits and don't make generalizations from a single experience – especially somebody else's experience. (One green skinned man once did you or your father or grandmother wrong, therefore, you decide all green skinned men are bad.)

I'm white. I've found that most white folks are good, law abiding, helpful, compassionate people. I've found a few that were out and out scoundrels. I've also found that most members of other races are good, law abiding, helpful, compassionate people. I've found a few of them to be out and out scoundrels, as well.

The point is obvious. Keep a cautious, open mind when you encounter 'Different' in any of its forms (people, ideas, methods ...). Explore what they have to offer. When you determine they are most likely danger free, embrace them and examine them; use what you find to expand your own possibilities for knowledge and Happiness. See what new truths you may discover. See what old 'truths' may be brought into question (provide opportunities for growth beyond what or where you are presently).

It is an obvious fact of life that some groups (primarily religions and cults – and recently some political orientations) expect (require) followers to reject all other differing philosophies. That often comes about because they are concerned that their own beliefs may not stand up to the test of comparison with others. It is at the base of much of the escalating hatred and violence in our world today.

Now let's turn our attention to Failure and Success. How many times did you get on and fall off a bike before you achieved easy, automatic, comfortable, riding, success? How many times did you attempt shoelace tying until you were able to accomplish it quickly, without even watching your fingers? How many times did you . . .?

Most of the skills that we have acquired down through the years have come through trial and error learning. Each time we try and fail we still do learn something that makes our next attempt come just a bit closer to success. (The learning guys call it skill acquisition through successive approximations, in case you're interested. I suppose they call it that even if you aren't interested. ☺)

So, praise be to all those failures!!! Without them where would any of us be? Most importantly, of course, we didn't give up through failure after failure after failure. We kept trying, utilizing what we learned from all those earlier attempts and pressing on. 'Failures' that, in fact, move us closer to success should be hailed and renamed – Hailures, perhaps!

I once had a friend who would always greet his own errors or mistakes or failures with the phrase, "Ah! Wonderful!" He was wisely celebrating the positive side of failure. I suggest you adopt his approach both when viewing your own mistakes and misjudgments, and those of others (friends, spouse, children, co-workers . . .). Point out to yourself what you learned - perhaps what not to do next time or perhaps what to hone or improve on just a bit next time.

When your child makes a mistake, has an accident, demonstrates poor judgment, or what have you, guide him to analyze how it came about and what needs to be changed or viewed differently so it won't need to happen again. (You noticed - I'm sure with no surprise - that I didn't mention setting a punishment for the miscue.) Help him learn to appreciate his honest mistakes. Help him appreciate his 'hailures'.

The important positive things the child receives from the use of that approach should be obvious. What about the parent? Happiness flows from that good match to his or her Positive Personal Philosophy of Living - "I want to be a helpful, compassionate person who does a good job of preparing my children for life beyond me."

Different doesn't necessarily mean bad, although it only makes good sense to use reasonable caution until you are satisfied it is safe. Reasonable failure should be welcomed as a positive, helpful, educational event. By 'reasonable' I refer to situations in which an activity has been approached with due deliberation and the best preparation you can make. To jump off a bridge wearing a pair of wings without first calculating weight to lift ratios and the required front to back wing curvature (from reliable sources) does not qualify as reasonable. To jump right into raising a child without studying what is known about child rearing is not reasonable. Investing in projects that you have not knowledgeably investigated is not reasonable. Alas (the old guy says), even from unreasonable failures some good can come; it is just that they too often also result in severe harm to some innocent person caught in the maelstrom of inadequate preparation. (The child raised in a family that has no inclination to learn what is known about raising kids appropriately, for example, is pretty well doomed to a life of unhappiness and probably fear.)

Where does all this lead us? First, always explore the new things that come your way (different) with open minded caution. People with a positive philosophy want to trust rather than distrust. Doing so, provides an integrity match which leads to Happiness. Outright rejection can never provide a match to any aspect of a positive philosophy of living.

It also points up the necessity for adequate preparation - training, education, practice, investigation - before undertaking a new project. In this day and age of instant access to information it should pose few problems. People who have a greater depth and breadth of knowledge are better prepared to meet the challenges of living. When opportunities to learn new things come your way, take advantage of them.

One of my daily goals is to never go to bed at night until I have learned something new and important that day. I'm flirting with eighty, have five earned college degrees, and still find myself wanting in terms of important pieces of information. Make the enjoyment of learning one of your positive goals. It will allow you to soar to new heights of knowledge. Knowledge is power when it comes to personal adjustment and Happiness.

I'll add one caution and stop the sermon! In your quest for knowledge make certain you are not only searching out data that support your beliefs, but more importantly investigate points of views that are at variance from your own. One can't truly grow intellectually so long as he keeps his search confined parochially within the limits of any personally accepted, predetermined, ideology. Unless our beliefs stand up to the most critical, open minded, evaluation, they probably need some honest 'growing'. (Think politics, think religion, think social philosophy.)

All of us have known people who react to failure or suggestions for change, with anger. I find anger to be a fully useless emotion and don't allow it, myself. If we approach and react to problems in the context of the Blame-Punish strategy, anger often accompanies it or follows it or re-ignites itself as we look back on it. To fully characterize that strategy, it needs to be extended in these ways:

A- Person One Blames and Punishes Person (or Group) Two.

B- Person Two, blames Person One for the discomfort or ego-bashing he administered and takes revenge back on him.

C- Person One then feels the need to Blame Person Two yet another time and he administers his own revenge.

D- Potentially, it never ends. Anger escalates at every interchange. Soon it becomes an irrational conflict between parties that just hate each other - fully divorced from the original problem.

My advice to parents has always been that they never try to figure out 'who started it' when interpersonal problems or disputes arise at home. "Bobby hit me." "Because you broke my pencil." "That was because you took my candy bar." "Well, last night you ate the last piece of pie." "Remember at the picnic last summer when you hogged all the chips?" and on and on and on until the day the younger one of them so ungraciously disrupted the family routine by being born!!!

The Blame-Punish strategy seldom really brings finality to any problem. It almost always brings continuing bad feelings.

When approaching life's problems from the Find Out and Fix Strategy, anger plays no role - there is no reason for it to ever come up. The sole aim is to solve the problem. What happened and what needs to be done so there is less likelihood that it will need to occur again?

One Christmas, a foster son who had been with us for less than two months made a gift in Woodshop for my wife and me. It was a routed wooden plaque that read: "No Blame Zone". That had never been put into words but compared with the home in which he had grown up I guess it seemed obvious to him. It soon rested in a place of honor above our front door.

Do away with the Blame-Punish Syndrome in your life and anger becomes a non-entity. Make your first response, "What needs to change here," and anger will never surface. Practice. Practice. Practice. (You still may have left over anger from past experiences. Discover those directives and get rid of them.)

Anger destroys individuals, families, nations, and lately it looks like it has a pretty good shot at destroying our World. Do your part to eliminate it.

EXERCISE:

Continue to refine your Daily Tune-Up so it concisely reflects the most important behaviors and points of view you want to display hour by hour as you proceed through your days. Resist the temptation to make that Daily Tune-Up statement too long or too complicated. Short, simple and precise are the keys. Remember, you can change it from day to day. Make sure that it is done daily!

Take time to evaluate how you are doing in a more general way. Are your behaviors matching the main (essential) elements of your Positive Personal Philosophy of living? Keep a list of those behaviors that seem inconsistent with your desires. Find their positive opposites and carefully build a Movie Screen replacement program.

When, after a week or so, one of the Directive Exchanges you worked on with the Movie Screen Technique appears to have not worked the way you had hoped, revisit the collages you created. Redesign them with more appropriate, intense, images. Add new images, perhaps. Make sure the two collages accurately represent opposite tendencies. During the exchange routine, spend more time with each collage – increase the intensity. I've never known the technique not to work when it was designed and administered appropriately.

CHAPTER THIRTEEN
SECRET 11
Focus on the Good Stuff

Thumper the Rabbit's mother said it best, perhaps. "If you don't have anything good to say about somebody, don't say anything at all." The only thing I can do to improve on that is to remind us all to apply it to ourselves as well as others. If I don't have anything good to say about myself, I won't say anything at all.

There are very few things that we think, say, or do that don't get stored in some fashion in our Deep Mind. People who dwell on the negative side of life fill their Deep Mind with a view of the world that poses a real threat for the Deep Mind. How can that be, you ask, if the Deep Mind refuses to accept negative directives?

Remember that Prime Directive - Keep my person safe. When the negatives appear to be life threatening (or comfort threatening) the Deep Mind does pay attention and does take immediate action.

When we paint a picture of a world filled with positive relationships and possibilities, the Deep Mind can relax, not needing to deal with threats. When we paint a picture of a world filled with unpleasant things the Deep Mind has to gear up to high alert as it prepares to deal with all those possible threats.

When the Deep Mind is kept busy spinning strategies to protect us, it becomes almost fully consumed by that job. Its other functions (services) immediately become less efficient and effective – less available. A person under such a siege has great difficulty maintaining his civil, helpful, compassionate, positive approach to living.

If you would take time to read the scientific studies that compare people's outlook on life with physical and mental disorders, you would be overwhelmed by the single truth that emerges. Folks who go through life dwelling on the negative and the potentially hurtful are many, many, many times more likely to develop serious illness and suffer emotional problems.

The lesson is clear: Approach living through a realistic, positive, philosophy and its resulting outlook, and your chances for good health, will surpass by many fold those who don't.

Let's examine some examples. In each case consider whether the Deep Mind is being washed with comfortable or uncomfortable data about the world and the people in it. I will present them as things said or thought.

> "The sun is shining. It's a beautiful day."
< "The sun is going to make it an unbearably hot and uncomfortable day today."

> "Maggie is dropping by. I hope I can put a smile on her face."
< "I wish Maggie weren't coming. She's the most depressing person I know."

> "I must write the Johnson's a note. Their precious son was killed in an accident last night."
< "Did you hear about that Johnson boy getting drunk again and causing that awful accident last night? It killed him and injured two passengers. I hear one of them may never play basketball again."

> This was said as a response to a rude clerk: "I hope the day begins going better for you."
< "You are the rudest store clerk I've ever encountered.

I'm going to report you to your supervisor!"

> "Pricilla sure has a style of her own."
< "Did you see that gosh awful getup Pricilla was wearing at the party last night?"

> "We played a good game regardless of the final score."
< "The Refs made bad calls against us all night!"
> "There is nothing we can do to change the final score, but I am so proud of the way you guys played tonight."
< "I feel like going and slitting the Ref's tires."

> "It looks like we get to re-bed the plants the trick or treaters trampled out there in our dark lawn last night."
< "I'm never going to treat those ungrateful little Blankity Blanks again."

I will guarantee that the folks with a bent toward the positive thoughts and statements left those situations feeling good inside. I will also guarantee that the folks with the blame-revenge thoughts and statements left the situations unhappier than ever.

As response patterns, Anger and Pleasure share one important trait; they both tend to linger and grow during the minutes and hours after they occur. Treat someone else in a pleasant way and the pleasure revisits you time and time again as you think back on it. Treat someone else in an angry (revenge based) way and that disagreeable, upsetting, feeling will continue to revisit you maintaining your anger.

It seems a no-brainer as the young folks say. We all want to feel happy (Happy!). There is such an easy formula available to make certain that happens and yet day in and day out so many folks just don't get it. Treat people (and yourself) positively, and good feelings flood your being. Treat people (and yourself) negatively, and you guarantee yourself an existence of continued, unpleasant, feelings.

Here is another set of well substantiated

characteristics: Intense pleasure gradually trails off into a warm, comfortable state of mind. Anger does not trail off. It builds and builds contributing to an even more unpleasant and inefficient condition. Why?

A pleasurable encounter has some finality to it. "We were nice to each other and the end result was this wonderful feeling." An angry encounter is never finished. Remember the Blame-Punishment paradigm? Angry encounters spiral into bigger and bigger confrontations - if only in one's mind. "He put me down and I'm going to get back at him, good!" The person then spends time planning anger-based, revenge taking, activities instead of letting it go and moving on.

When an unpleasant comment would grace my lips, Mom said, "Bite your tongue." Taking her at her word, as a four-year-old, I tried it. Far too painful and excessively bloody, I discovered. Although I never discussed it with Mom, I replaced her saying with my own less painful one. "Plant a smile."

When I got the urge to have an unkind thought or make an unkind (never helpful) remark, I bypassed the teeth-to-tongue thing and broke a grin. That grin soon became a signal to my Deep Mind to send all kinds of good feelings into my being. It started me on my exploration of the mind-body connection. In my book on Deep Mind Mastery I present a number of body positions (referred to as Stances) one can practice that immediately signal the Deep Mind to flood your body with certain kinds of feelings (one for power, one for contentment, one for courage, one for patience, and so on).

If I were to ask you to form your body into a position similar to that maintained by a depressed, clearly unhappy person, what would you do? I imagine you would drop your head, lower your shoulders, dangle your arms limply at your sides, droop your eyes, frown just a bit, and probably even without prompting, sigh deeply. If you hold that position for long you WILL begin feeling down about things - blue. It is one of the universal mind-body connections.

Change that position into shoulders back, chin up, arms bent at the elbows, a modest smile on your face, eyes wide open and looking from place to place, and you have immediately changed your mood (your outlook) into a more powerful, in-control, ready to act, positive stance.

I seem to be into sayings, here. "Smile and the world smiles with you." "Laughter is contagious."

The human mind is designed to want to smile and laugh and feel a positive rush (by whatever name). When the situation seems right for that (seeing others smiling or laughing) the mind rushes to join in. There are few things that signal safety to the Deep Mind more than smiles and laughter. Would you prefer to go to a performance by a comic or a gloom and doom dispenser? Would you rather come home at night to a smiling, laughing, family (that you helped create) or a sullen, upset group of folks (that, maybe, you helped create)?

Let me try one more saying: "I'm high on life." It has been maligned and ridiculed and put down by those who don't understand it - who live their lives according to negative philosophies and the blame-punish strategy. It is perhaps the best test of all: If one dismisses the saying, he clearly is not on the positive track. If one accepts it or even nods a slight recognition of its possible truth, his tendency is toward a positive philosophy and way of living.

So, a sure way to keep oneself angry and stirred up, in a personally destructive negative sense, is to focus on the negative. A sure way to keep oneself happy and Happy and hopeful about mankind and the Planet is to focus on the positive.

Does this mean positive folks deny the negative aspects of life? Most certainly not. But the positive person evaluates each negative situation by asking if dwelling on it holds any potential for fixing it, or spreading happiness, contentment, and good will. If it doesn't, then they acknowledge its existence but let it go. Do I watch evening newscasts, which are filled to overflowing with all that has gone wrong in the world that day? I do, but its purpose for me is to keep me informed not to keep me depressed or angry at the 'bad guys'. If a story appears to hold promise of new information, I watch it. If it doesn't, I put the set on mute and await the next story. During mute, I water my plants, dust, pick up my living room, and such. (I've even been known to do something resembling push-ups and squat thrusts! Ugh!)

I believe that folks who purport to be good folks should put their money and energy where their mouth is. I particularly believe that's true for authors and speakers who make proposals like those in this book. In general, I am fully private about my 'good works' (for lack of a better expression). Like my Dad said, I believe they should be done anonymously whenever possible. But for purposes of illustration let me open my life to you just a crack.

I'm concerned about poverty and hunger. It is a worldwide phenomenon but there is little I can do about it in Africa or Afghanistan or India. I can, however, do something about it here in my own community. I don't dwell on the sad and despairing side of the issue. I dwell on the fact that I am doing things to alleviate the pain in whatever ways I can. The negative situation is certainly there, but I spend my mental and emotional energy examining the improvement and the increasing joy and comfort I can provide. Years ago, I gave up vacations in order to use that money to accomplish things that I believe are really important for improving the lot of mankind.

Many positive contributions cost nothing at all, of course. Volunteering would be one such undertaking. Churches, the Salvation Army, libraries, schools, hospitals, adult education centers, senior care services, meals-on-wheels, food pantries, the Red Cross, Habitat for Humanity, The Muscular Dystrophy and Childhood Diabetes Associations, Literacy initiatives, safe houses, after school care programs, and the like all need and welcome helping hands.

EXERCISE:

Begin another list. (You'd think I owned stock in the yellow pad company, wouldn't you!) On this one, place ideas about things you can do that will be above and beyond your usual activities. They must show good promise of helping some part of humanity right there in your city, town, community, or neighborhood (family, even). Then take the action step and get it on your calendar. If you need further information, make the call or go on the internet. One such activity on your calendar for every week will be a good starting place. Configure it as a win-win activity - somebody else benefits and you find a match to some part of your Positive Personal Philosophy of Living. You can do the same thing week after week or try several until you get a feel for what works best for you and the others.

I know a grandma in Florida who makes herself available on her front porch to read to lower grade kids after school. The stoop is packed most every day.

I know a man who fixed up part of his garage as a bicycle shop and helps youngsters maintain and repair their bikes there Saturday mornings.

I know a couple who open their pool to kids from an inner-city program Sunday afternoon.

I know an old man in Minnesota whose one claim to fame is whittling. After school the door to his basement is open for anyone who wants to watch or learn (parental permission required of course here, like in most of these situations).

I know a teen boy (star athlete) who volunteers after school in a seventh-grade reading room to help boys improve their skills and become interested in all the wonderful things books can offer them.

I know a mechanic who spends one morning a week helping Seniors at their social center solve and fix car problems from fuses to oil changes.

Why do these folks keep doing these things week after week, year after year? You know the answer, of course. Because of the wonderful doses of Deep Down Forever Happiness their activities bring their way.

Helping is not undertaken to make yourself or others look upon you as a good person. It is done because it needs to be done and that is what good people do.

Integrity. Living a life in which one's daily activities match one's positive goals and values.

Since I haven't seemed able to pass up a good saying in this chapter, let's end with a slightly remodeled version of a not too long ago famous one: Integrity - Don't leave home without it!

CHAPTER FOURTEEN
SECRET 12
Downsize the Stuff in Your Life

The suggestions in this chapter begin from a Positive Personal and Social Philosophy of Living, which suggests that all one really needs for Deep Down Forever Happiness is maintaining ones Integrity. Anything else, above the necessities of life, are unnecessary. It doesn't mean you may not decide to keep some of the fun stuff. Here we will try to put Stuff, Power, Prestige, Money, Fame, and Self-esteem into perspective.

One basic rule of downsizing is this: If you got something for the purpose of increasing your standing with others, you don't need it. Elaborated it becomes: if you have, or do, or seek, anything for the sole purpose of enhancing your status, power, prestige, fame, or self-esteem, consider giving it up. A life driven by a Positive Philosophy doesn't need outside verification of its goodness or appropriateness or importance. It receives that verification every time a deed is felt to be a match with a positive value or goal.

I often ask young people if they would rather be rich or happy. The answer is surprisingly consistent. "I'd rather be rich because then I'd be happy." They think they have tricked me. Actually, and unfortunately, they have tricked themselves.

What a malevolent disservice our culture is doing for these youngsters.

In the area of finding Happiness and self-esteem, our

culture has effectively turned reality upside down - largely due to the efforts of Madison Avenue advertising executives, I suspect. Quite consistently their bottom line is monetary profit. Money over positive values. Money over human decency. Money now over long-term planetary considerations. Virtually nothing else is ever considered. Their very effective marketing strategy is simple: In order to be happy, to retain or regain your youthful appearance, to let others know you are successful, and to fit in socially, you have to own this product. It is as if they believe none of us ever mature beyond the Jr. High - "I have to fit in" - mentality. Perhaps most of us don't. The sales strategy continues to be extremely successful generation after generation.

It is a strategy that has to fail with folks driven by a positive philosophy of life because the basic motivators, with which the advertisers play, hold no power (success; social acceptance; perennial youth, and stuff-based happiness - all frequently equated with sex).

Be Happy with yourself and your life FIRST. Then, decorate your life with functional stuff - beautiful, quality, functional stuff, even. But NOT status-providing stuff or other stuff that is purchased for the purpose of making you Happy. It doesn't work.

You will remember the differentiation we made between Happiness and the more momentary, fun and pleasurable aspects of living. You will remember also that I believe Fun and Pleasures are important parts of lives. One difference I have with some folks is about what it takes to have fun. I tend to forget that many people believe they have to have things and gadgets and travel and entertainment presented by others to have fun. Because I'm so regularly filled with warm fuzzies from my contacts with people I don't think about those things. I don't have time for that stuff. I believe that most folks who are actively committed to living a life based on a Positive Philosophy have little need - little time - for all the entertaining stuff.

Downsizing becomes so simple when one bases his source for happiness in maintaining that deed/value match. Anything else seems so artificial - superfluous.

Why downsize? It requires less energy, time, and money for starters. Without those reminders of unnecessary excess, it is easier for your Deep Mind to understand that such excesses are no longer among your priorities. It sends a complicated mixed signal when you tell it one thing but show it something different. Like a child, the Deep Mind will believe the 'image' over the words almost every time.

A true case.

'Tom' and 'Sara' were in their early forties and had been married 18 years. In high school, he had been the all-round athletic hero and she the head cheerleader and beauty queen. He came back home after college and became the golf pro at the local Country Club. Sara operated a card and gift shop. They had a son, Rick, 16 and a daughter, Amber, 12. Their combined income was well above average for their community of 100,000. Prestige and fame continued to be their goals. They had three cars and two ATVs parked in the garage of their twelve-room house, a 22-foot boat in the driveway, a swimming pool, a spa, a tennis court, tanning beds, and a time share condo in Los Vegas. Amber was failing several classes. Rick had been arrested for driving under the influence the second week he had his license and his new car (after a life-long bout with misbehavior). The family finances were in trouble. The tension between Tom and Sara mounted and they were investigating a divorce.

Enter downsizing. They were desperate and willing to try almost anything to get their lives back on track. After a month in counseling aimed at developing a positive philosophy for the family - all members participated - tensions eased dramatically. Rick had the most problems with the undertaking but even he eventually became fruitfully engaged in the endeavor.

Six months later they were in a smaller (though large enough) house, were down to two cars (and cooperative transportation schedules), found they could do without the boat, pool and tennis courts, and all of them spent lots more time at home. Rick and Amber 'remolded' the basement into a place they and their friends could hang out. They established and posted a list of expected behaviors from those who utilized their hospitality. After the first boy was asked not to come back (by Rick) there were few more infringements of the rules.

The prospect of divorce had long since passed. Tom began giving free golf lessons one afternoon a week for kids who couldn't afford them. Sara and Amber organized an ongoing entertainment series for a Senior Center. Rick assisted with a Cub Scout Pack. They fixed and ate the evening meal together and found they actually had lots of important and interesting things to talk about. The parents learned to become good listeners and surprisingly the kids did, too.

I could go on but the point has been made. The final time I saw the family the boy made an interesting, insightful comment that moistened all the other eyes in the room. "You know, we should have junked that big house years ago." I still hear from that boy several times a year. He's a daddy now, living a very Happy, simple, ever-helpful, life according to his epistles.

When contemplating downsizing, perhaps the best question to ask is, "How simple can I (we) make my life and still be Happy, happy, and well cared for?" When that question is asked from the perspective of a successful, Positive Personal Philosophy, you can bet the resulting lifestyle will be a whole lot simpler than most people seem to feel they need these days.

When I ask adult folks what the number one problem is in their life (aside from money) the answer is almost universally, "It's just too hectic."

"And how does that come about?"

"Just working everything we have to do into the schedule."

"Such as?"

"Lisa's dance and gymnastics and cheer leading. Billy's sports and band and scouts and BMX. All their homework every night. Jack and my card party night, my PTO work, our jobs, Jack's golfing and Little League coaching, and so on."

I'm worn out. How about you?

The less affluent are more tuned into work related

problems. "I'm working full time and my husband is working two jobs. The car is a constant worry and we just keep shuffling through our bills paying minimums on everything. The kids aren't doing well in school and my boy stays out way later than he should at night. I don't know his friends, but I hear they are mostly troublemakers. I'm exhausted all the time and none of us ever sees my husband."

Back in the late nineteen sixties there was a wonderful book in wide circulation titled, "Let Children Be Children". It was co-authored by a Social Worker (Dr. Freda Kim or Kehm, perhaps) and a school superintendent (Joe Mini). Its premise was that kids only have one chance to be kids so we should reorganize the expectations families, schools, and society make on them, so they have time to just be themselves. They advocated far less homework and organized out of the home activities, suggesting that when schoolwork, sports, and other activities become the recognized bottom line for successful child rearing (childhood) something is clearly messed up - and in a most devastating way!

Childhood should be about learning to appreciate the family, learning to love themselves and others, inculcating compassion and selfless helpfulness into their approach to living, and locating and pursuing their individual strengths and passions.

I'll tell you for sure that when success ceases to be defined in terms of fame, fortune, and furniture, and instead is seen as love, self-esteem, and a desire to help all of mankind, life turns around beautifully (as does the prospect for a wonderful future for the human species).

In many ways, it is really a matter of replacing competition with cooperation. If not replacing competition, at least getting the scale back into some kind of reasonable balance. I cringe when I hear that young boys have personal coaches to hothouse their athletic skills. Clearly the bottom line in those families is not to let children be children. The bottom line has become athletic success above a youngster's (a family's) overall well-being. (I hear ten thousand, angry, bat wielding, fathers marching toward my Ozark home! I can smell the acrid blame and punish mentality rushing on ahead of them.)

I enjoy watching kids being let off at and picked up from school. Some parents are clearly put out by having to wait an extra minute while their children have a few parting words with their friends. They stay in the car, honking or revving the engine. Some call out in unpleasant tones.

Others park the car and go to meet their children. They clearly know the friends and have a cordial interchange before walking their son or daughter to the car, arms around each other's waists chatting about whatever.

I once worked with a twelve-year-old boy. He had a HUGE problem that was - he thought - absolutely ruining his life. When his Dad let him off at school in the morning, they kissed each other on the cheeks. The other boys had begun teasing him about it. As we talked, two alternatives emerged for him. One, he could explain the situation to his father who, we both knew, would stop the routine in favor of his son's happiness. Second, he and his father could continue to express their love for each other in that way and the boy would need to find ways of handling it with his friends. As we talked, he came to feel bad for his friends who were unable to express their feelings openly like that.

The next week he came into my office all smiles.

"So?" I asked.

"I didn't say anything to Dad. When the boys began making their remarks, I asked them, 'Don't you guys love your Dads?' They haven't said anything since. Now, about Emily - this girl I'd really, really, like to . . ."

The boy had opted for Deep Down Happiness and Integrity, by doing what he thought was right. It may not seem to have much to do with downsizing, but I'll tell you, when one's level of Integrity and Positive Philosophy of Living is as strong as that boy's, downsizing will become a cinch! He did what he believed was the right thing to do and in order to remain true to himself he was willing to live with the unpredictable consequences from his friends. Many would call him brave. (In Jr. High, it was probably outrageously courageous!)

All of that started as an example of parents needing to

allow a few extra minutes in their daily schedule so the usual rush, rush, rush, approach will not be necessary. A schedule should never be constructed so it becomes more important than people. Downsizing the time squeeze is often a necessary and welcome change.

Make another list - a huge list - of the things you have and do and want. Just a random list assembled as things come to mind. Give yourself a week or so to complete it. Then, begin scanning through it at least once a day. Each time you come to something that doesn't contribute in any significant way to your Deep Down Happiness (doesn't make a match with one of your Positive values) put a check in front of it (don't mark it out, yet). Later, begin putting an X in front of those entries that cause you unnecessary frustration or consume time and energy you'd rather be using in some other way (no fair Xing your kids or relatives!). (Some items may have both a check and an X.)

Set it aside for a week or so and then go back to it. If your spouse did the same exercise, he or she should do it separately from you. Later, mark through the items you can easily do without. Make a note behind each about how you will continue to fill the needs you may have thought it was fulfilling (if those needs actually exist anymore). Eventually compare notes with your spouse. Talk! Share ideas and feelings (in your no blame zone!).

Bottom line. If something is causing or maintaining tension and does not really reflect a match with any of your Positive Values, consider letting it go. I imagine you might be surprised at how many families I know who have been able to reduce their work hours dramatically and find they actually have more money at their disposal once they downsized in a comfortable way. The charities they chose were grateful.

You will find a variety of books available at your bookstore (I hope you have 'your' bookstore) on the topic of downsizing. Some are written from the greedy point of view (save money here so you will have more to spend for something else you want to possess) but many come from a more altruistic point of view. (The catch phrases on the covers usually distinguish them at a glance.)

If I have a formula to use it goes like this.

Determine what stuff and activities you really need in order to be Happy (I'm sure you'll find that most of what you have and much of what you do, play no part in Happy.)

Determine what kinds of alternative activities you can engage in that will bring you both happiness and Happiness but have a far smaller price tag. [Family at home together-times; volunteer time - perhaps together as a family, even; re-establishing regular contacts with relatives and old friends; opening your house a few hours a week to young teens or seniors (or both at the same time!).]

Do your elimination of excesses. (It may well involve the downsizing of big possessions like houses and extra vehicles as well as trinkets and baubles.)

Determine how you are going to use all the excess money and time you find you have. (Remember, I came from a relatively money poor home and we still managed ten percent of our earnings to help those who we saw as the less fortunate.)

If you find yourself already downsized by catastrophe or what seems to be your lot in life, don't think you have to cut out anything. Downsizing is for those who let the stuff and social pressures in their lives get way out of control.

In either case, revisit your Positive Personal and Social Philosophy of Living every week or so to see if it needs adjusting (additions or deletions) or just shake it up a bit if some of those less relevant directives have moved into cubby holes that should be reserved for more important values and endeavors.

CHAPTER FIFTEEN
SUMMARY

Short, repetitive, books, like this one, probably don't require summaries and I intended this to be a short, to the point, teaching, manual. My suggestion is that you re-read it several times. As a way of review and summary let me ask some questions. They are generally listed in the order in which they were discussed in the book. Fearlessly try for an answer before you peek. Remember, failure is nothing more than a helpful guidepost!

> Contrast Altruism and Selfism.

> What is the difference between happiness and Happiness as used in this manual?

> Never let your expectations for Deep Down Forever Happiness flow from _____.

> Contrast a Positive Philosophy of living with a non-positive philosophy.

> List the six to ten top priority values in your Positive Philosophy of Living.

> Define Integrity: A match between ...

> Should you take good care of yourself or others? (a trick question!)

> Replace worrying with _____.

> Replace the (BAP) _____ and _____ technique with the (FOF) ___ ___ and ___ technique.

> Anger is a natural outcome of which technique mentioned above?

> Compassion and helpfulness are the natural outcomes of which technique?

> Teach yourself to see Failures and Mistakes as _____.

> In general, only relate and dwell on _____ things about yourself and others.

> D_____ize the stuff and excess activities in your life. Use the extra time and money to _____ the human species.

> When you continue to behave in a way that you don't want to behave, it probably represents an unwanted Deep Mind D_____ive. Choose one to _____ it and use the M____ie Th_____er technique to make the switch.

> When the author is limited to making just one suggestion for a family in stress, he often tells them to begin f_xing and e_ting me_ls together at least six times a week.

A young reporter once asked me what I wanted inscribed on my tombstone. I thank him for that question because since then I have often asked others the same thing. It requires us to condense into just a few words how we want to be remembered throughout all eternity. I find it a sobering way of quickly putting a lifetime into perspective.

If one chooses something like, "I was beautiful," or "I won because I ended up with the most expensive toys," then I shed tears for her or him because both have so sadly missed the precious, unique, essence of their human potential.

My answer to the young reporter: "Every day I set out to make the World a better place."

I wish the same for you and I wish you Deep Down Forever Happiness. Most likely they are all a part of the same package, aren't they?

HAVE A WONDER FILLED, DEEP DOWN HAPPY, LIFE